PREFACE

The Revolutionary records contained in this volume were compiled from the Court records of Lancaster County, Virginia. The records prior to 1800 have recently been moved to Richmond, and are in the State Archives. Those after 1800 are still in the County Clerk's Office.

The records include the recommendation of the Court of those qualified to serve as officers in the County Militia, a record of their qualifications, certification of the heirs of a deceased soldier or sailor, tracing the descent for three and sometimes four generations, movements of troops, public service claims &c. The records also include the date of birth and death of many of the soldiers, also a number of marriages for which there are no bonds or other records.

This volume also includes the Master Rolls and Pay Rolls of the Ninety-second Regiment of Virginia Militia, Lancaster County, War of 1812, commanded by Lt. Col. John Chowning, of those entitled to Land Bounty under Act of Congress of 28 September, 1850. These were copied from Rolls in the Auditor's Office, Richmond, Virginia, and published by the Government in 1851.

* Indicated that the same name appears more than once on the same page.

The compiler wishes to acknowledge his sincere appreciation to Mr. Oscar B. Chilton, Clerk, and to Rev. L. R. Combs, of the many courtesies extended him not only while engaged in making these abstracts, but upon every occasion when good fortune takes him to Lancaster Court House.

REVOLUTIONARY SOLDIERS AND SAILORS
from
LANCASTER COUNTY
V I R G I N I A

Muster Rolls and Pay Rolls
of the
Ninety-Second Regiment
of Virginia Militia
Lancaster County
1812

ᚼᚼ

Compiled by
Stratton Nottingham

HERITAGE BOOKS
2012

HERITAGE BOOKS
AN IMPRINT OF HERITAGE BOOKS, INC.

Books, CDs, and more—Worldwide

For our listing of thousands of titles see our website
at
www.HeritageBooks.com

A Facsimile Reprint
Published 2012 by
HERITAGE BOOKS, INC.
Publishing Division
100 Railroad Ave. #104
Westminster, Maryland 21157

Originally published 1930

— Publisher's Notice —
In reprints such as this, it is often not possible to remove blemishes from the original. We feel the contents of this book warrant its reissue despite these blemishes and hope you will agree and read it with pleasure.

International Standard Book Numbers
Paperbound: 978-1-58549-395-1
Clothbound: 978-0-7884-9132-0

Orders - July 1770 to 1778 - (15)

At a Court held for Lancaster County on the 18th day of July, 1776, In Pursuance of the Ordinances of the general Convention of this Colony of Virginia, being the first Court held for the said County after the Establishment of the new Form of Government in this Colony & the Declaration of Congress for the Independence of the American States.

James Ball first Justice having taken the oath prescribed by the Convention, administered the same to John Chinn, Edwin Conway, Jesse Ball, James Selden, Hugh Brent, John Taylor, Thomas Lawson & James Gordon, Gent: who took their Seats in Court.

Thomas B. Griffin qualified Clerk of the said Court by taking the Oath directed by Ordinance, also Richard Mitchell, Gent: high Sheriff, Joseph Shearman & Bailie George Deputy Sheriffs: David Boyd, William Broun & Richard E. Lee Attornies and Spencer George & Michael Wilder Constables. p. 414

"Jesse Ball, Gent: is by the Court recommended to his Excellency the Governor as a proper person to execute the Office of Colo. of the Militia in this County in the room of Thadeus MacCarty, who has removed.

Thomas B. Griffin is recommended to be Lieutenant Colo. in the Room of Colo. Jesse Ball.

John Taylor, Gent: is recommended to be Major of the sd Militia in the Place of James Selden, Gent: decd" 20 Mar. 1777 - p. 419

"Thomas Carter is recommended as a Person qualified to be Captain of the Militia in this County in the Room of Henry Lawson who has resigned & Isaac Degges for Lieutenant in the Place of the said Carter" 18 Apr. 1777 - p. 421

"Jesse Ball, Gent. produced a Common from his Excellency the Governor appointing him Colo. of the Militia of this County, Thomas B. Griffin to be Lieutenant Colo. & John Taylor, Gent. Major, they each severally qualified to their respective Common by taking all the Oaths prescribed by Ordinance for the same" 15 May, 1777 - p. 423

"John Fleet, James Gordon, Thomas Lawson & John Berryman, Gent. are appointed by the Court to tender the Oath or Affirmation for Giving Assurance of Allegiance to this State & the other American States, in the lower Part of this County; John Taylor, Gent. for the Parish of Wiccomico, and Henry Tapscott, Henry Towles & James Ball, Jr. for the same Purpose in the upper Part of this County." 17 July, 1777 - p. 425

"William Chowning, James Ewell, Bailie George, Thomas

Hathaway & Richard Selden are nominated & recommended to his Excellency Patrick Henry, Esqr. as fit & able Persons to execute the Office of Lieutenants in the Militia of this County, also William Gibson & Elias Edmonds Ensigns in the s^d Militia" 21 Aug. 1777 - p. 426

"Thomas Carter qualified to a Captain's Commission, Isaac Deggs, Richd Selden & Thomas Hathaway Lieutenants & John Chowning Ensign in the Militia of this County by taking the Oaths prescribed by Ordinance" 16 Oct. 1777 - p. 428

Orders - 1778 to 1783 - (16)

"John Taylor, gent: is by the Court recommended to his Excellency the Governor as a Person Qualified to be Lieutenant of this County; Edwin Conway, gent: Colonel; James Gordon, gent: Lieut: Colonel; James Ball, Jr., gent: Major; John Bailey Capt. in the room of James Ball, Jr., Isaac Deege Capt. in the room of William Yerby, and Lawson Hathaway Second Lieutenant in Capt. Thomas Carter's Company" 20 Aug. 1778 - p. 12

"John Taylor, Gen^t: sworn County Lieutenant, Edwin Conway Colonel, James Gordon, Gen^t: sworn Lieutenant Colonel, James Ball, Jr. Major, Isaac Degge Captain Third Company; John Bailey Captain of the fourth Company, John Chowning second Lieutenant to Capt. Bailey's Company, Edward Blakemore Ensign to the same & Lawson Hathaway second Lieutenant to Capt Carter's Company of the Militia of this County agreeable to their respective Commissions by taking the usual Oaths to the Commonwealth" 15 Oct. 1778 - p. 15

"James Ewell is by the Court recommended to his Excellency the Governor as a proper person to act as a Captain of the Militia in the room of Capt Robert Chinn who resigned, and Rawleigh Tapscott appointed to act as second Lieut: of the said Company" 15 Oct. 1778 - p. 17

"James Ewell produced a Commission from his Excellency the Governor appointing him Captain of the Militia of this County, who by taking the necessary Oath is quallifyed to act accordingly" 19 Nov. 1778 - p. 20

"Richard Selden and William Gibson are by the Court recommended to his Excellency the Governor as proper persons to act as Captains in the Militia of this County, Elias Edmonds and Lott Palmer as Lieutenants and James Pollard Ensign" 19 Nov. 1778 - p. 21

"On the motion of Isabel Kent, widow of Jesse Kent, who Died in the service of this State, Ordered the Treasurer pay to John Berryman, Gent: for the support of the said Kent's Family, the sum of Fifty pounds current money" 17 Dec. 1778 - p. 22

"On the motion of Hannah Thatcher whose Husband Died in the Service of this State, Ordered the Treasurer pay to John Berryman, Gent: for the support of her family the sum of Thirty pounds Current Money" 17 Dec. 1778 - p. 22

"On the motion of Milly Galloway, whose Husband Died in the Service of this Continent, Ordered the Treasurer pay to Richard Mitchell, Gent: for her use the sum of Thirty pounds Current Money" 17 Dec. 1778 - p. 22

"On the motion of Leannah Overstreet, whose Husband died in the service of this State, ordered the Treasurer pay to John Berryman, Gent: the sum of Fifty pounds for her use" 18 Mar. 1779 - p. 25

"William Gibson and Richard Selden Qualifyed as Captains of the Militia; John Chowning sworn Lieutenant and James Pollard Ensign.
William Kirk is appointed Ensign to the third Company of this Militia.
William Kirk sworn Ensign to the third Company of Militia" 15 Apr. 1779 - p. 27

"Lott Palmer took the necessary oath to qualify him to act as Lieutenant to the 5th Company of the Militia, also Edward Blakemore as Ensign to the 4th Company.
Ordered the Treasurer pay to Henry Lawson, Gent: the Sum of £50 for the Support of Rachel Hill whose husband died in the Navy service of this State" 20 May, 1779 - p. 28

"Elijah Percifull took the oath prescribed to Quallify himself to act as an Ensign in the Militia of this County" 8 June, 1779 - p. 31

"Ordered the Clerk certify to the Auditors of this State that Jesse Kent died about May, 1778, in the Navy service of the said State and has left a Widow and five children.

William Smith who is now in the service of this State, and having a family consisting of a Wife and three children, is by this Court allowed four Barrels of Corn and two hund: pounds of Pork for their support, and it is ordered to be certified to the Auditors that Pork is selling at £50 p^r ₵^{t} & Corn at £30 p^r Br^l.

Ordered the Clerk certify to the Auditors of this State that William Thatcher died about March 177- in the Navy service of the said State and has left a Widow and two children"   20 Apr. 1780 - p. 46

"At a Court held at Lancaster Court House on Monday the 5th day of February 1781 Pursuant to an Act of the General Assembly entitled an Act for supplying the Army with Cloths, Provisions and Waggons

Pres^t (James Ball   John Taylor   James Ball,Jr.)
(John Fleet   James Gordon   Henry Lawson) Gen^t Jus-
(Richard Mitchell Henry Towles   And   ) tices
(Edwin Conway   William Yerby   John Selden   )

Who contracted with John McTyre of the aforesaid County for a Waggon Complete with Two Horses and Harness for Four, and James Ball, Gent: is appointed to purchase the other Two Horses for the said Waggon   Signed by
                                      Ja^s Ball" - p. 73

"Bailie George is recommended to his Excellency Thomas Nelson, Esqr, Governor of Virginia as a proper person to act as first Lieutenant, William Kirk second Lieutenant and John Flowers Ensign to Capt Gibson's Company; Lott Palmer first and Presly Saunders second Lieutenants to Capt Selden's Company in this Militia"   21 June 1781 - p. 79

"James Gordon, Gent: is recommended to his Excellency Thomas Nelson, Esqr Governor of Virginia as a proper person to act as Colonel of this County in the room of Edwin Conway, Gent: who resigned, James Ball, Jr. to succeed James Gordon as Lieutenant Col. of the Militia of Lancaster"   19 July, 1781 - p. 80

"Thomas Pollard, Gent: presented a Commission from his Excellency Thomas Jefferson, Esqr appointing him Captain of the Company of Cavalry of this County. Newton Brent presented a Commission also appointing him Lieutenant of the said Company, and John Sullivant Cornett to the same, who Quallified to the same accordingly"   19 July 1781 - p. 80

"Henry Towles, Gent: is recommended to his Excellency Thos Nelson Esqr Governor of Virginia as a proper person to execute the office of a Major in this Militia in the room of James Ball, Jr."   16 Aug. 1781 - p. 81

"Edwin Conway, Gent: is recommended to his Excellency the Governor of Virginia as a proper person to execute the office of a

Cornet for this County in the room of Richd Mitchell, Gent: dec^d."
15 Nov. 1781 - p. 85

"Rawleigh Tapscott, who acted as Deputy Commissioner under the appointment of Mr John Brown, Commissioner, for the State of Virginia, received a Waggon and Four Horses, Pursuant to an Act of the General Assembly Intitled an Act for supplying the Army with Cloths, Provisions and Waggons, and he the said Tapscott being charged by this Court with a breach of his duty, produced a Receipt from M^r. Nat. Nason Q. M. Brigade for the delivery of the said Waggon &c, Whereupon it is ordered that the said Receipt together with a letter from the said Brown to the said Tapscott be entered upon record and certified by the Clerk of the Court to the Auditor of Public Accounts, which is as follows:

Richmond, Feby 8th, 1781.

Sir: Having been honoured with the appointment of Commissioner for the State of Virginia with powers to appoint an Assistant in ⓞ County, I have taken the liberty to appoint you for the County of Lancaster, not doubting but your Zeal for the public good will induce you to accept of the appointment. Your duty is partly pointed out in the Act of Assembly and other papers inclosed; as soon as the Waggons, Boats &c. are entered with you, you will transmit an account of the numbers with the Proprietors names, to enable me to comply with the order of the Executive, in laying them of in -Brigades, you must keep exact accounts of all certificates granted, to whom, for what and the amount. I have this day received orders from the Executive to collect all the Beef Cattle &c. & also a number of Cattle for the purpose of Stalling; this business I would wish you to lose no time in executing this business, & in order to do justice as near as possible, I would advise you to the following method which has been adopted in some Counties, which I think a just one; to take a Tenth part of the Stock of Cattle, & as some Counties have furnished a number of Cattle already, I think it reasonable the persons who have furnished a Tenth should be excused, & the Cattle now to be taken from those persons that have not furnished their proportion, which will leave no room for complaint; as there is no Law for taking poor Cattle & the Ascertaining the Weight of them in that condition would be doing injustice to the holders, I think they ought to be adjudged supposing the Cattle to be good Grease Beef, the Cattle as fast as collected you will put in the hands of good men to have Stalled, furnish them with Forage which you must procure agreeable to the last Act of Assembly, as you will have the direction of the Grain Tax within your County, I am in hopes you will be able to furnish grain for the Stalling of them Cattle without application to the Act of Assembly for that Article. You are also to give Immediate notice to the Court of your County, that you will receive the Waggon Teams & other Appendages that is to be found by your County agreeable to an Act of the last Assembly, which you are to deliver to the nearest Continental Quarter Master, taking his Receipt, and forward me a Certificate of the Cost of the Waggon Team &c. in order that the Continent be Debited with the amount. You

will be allowed for your trouble Four Thousand pounds of Tobacco p^r year or its worth in paper money according to the Valuation made by the Grandjury at the Court next before the date of your Warrant.
I am respectfully
Sir -
Your most Obe: Servant
John Brown, Commissioner
for the State of Virg^a

P^s: As you may be at a loss what allowance to make the persons you employ to stall the Cattle, I advise you to submit it to the Court of your County what they shall receive for their trouble.
J. B.

To Mr Rawleigh Tapscott,
Lancaster.

Rec^d August 19th 1781 of Mr Rawleigh Tapscott One Waggon and Four Horses, publick property -
Nat. Nason Q. M. Brigade

At a Court held for Lancaster County the 12th day of March, 1782 - This Letter, together with the Receipt, was ordered to be recorded
Test: Thad^s McCarty, Cl.Cur." -
p. 91

"James Gordon, James Ball, Jr. and Henry Towles, Gent: qualified to their respective Commissions in this Militia, to-wit: James Gordon Colonel, James Ball, Jr. Lieut: Colonel and Henry Towles Major by taking the oath prescribed by Law" 18 Apr. 1782 - p. 94

"Bailie George sworn First Lieutenant, William Kirk second & John Flowers Ensign to the Third Company of this Militia by taking the Oath prescribed by Law" 19 Apr. 1782 - p. 95

"The Court then proceeded to receive the different Certificates and Accounts for claims against the publick agreeable to an Act of Assembly Intitled an Act for Adjusting Claims for property Impress'd or taken for publick service, to-wit:

To John Chinn, Gent: for one Bay Horse 14½ hands high 11 years old Impress'd by Nicholas Currell by Order of Col. William Griffin in October 1781	30 - 0 - 0
N° 5 To d^o for Beef Imp. by Raw^h Tapscott D. C. for John Brown in May 1781	7 - 5 - 0
112 To D^o for d^o d^o Oc^r 1781	14 -10 - 0
To D^o for 20 Gallons Brandy Imp. by Saml Guthrie by Ord. of Col. John Taylor in September 1781 @ 9/	9 - 0 - 0
To D^o for 17½^{lb} Bacon Furnished the Guards in Octr 1781	11 - 8
	61 - 6 - 8

"To the Reverd Mr David Currie for a Gray Horse 14 hands
high 11 years old Imp. by Nicholas Currell by order
of Col. William Griffin in September 1781   20 - 0 - 0
89 To Do for Beef Imp. by Rawh Tapscott D. C. for John
Brown in Ocr 1781   10 - 0 - 0
    30 - 0 - 0

To John Hill Carter Esqr for a Gray Horse 15 Hands high
13 years old Imp. by Nicholas Currell by order of Col.
William Griffin in Septr 1781   30 - 0 - 0
To Do for 1 Bay do 14 hands high 20 years old Imp. by
Do   Do   5 - 0 - 0
45 To Do for Beef Imp. by Rawh Tapscott D. Com. for John
Brown in July 1781   50 -15 - 0
To Do for Mutton & Lamb furnished the Guards in June 1781   2 -12 - 0
To Do for 6 Muttons furnished the Prison Guards in do @ 10/   3 - 0 - 0
    99 - 7 - 0

To Col. John Taylor for 1 Sorrel Horse 14 hands high 11
years old Imp. by Nicholas Currell by order of Col.
William Griffin in Septr 1781   20 - 0 - 0

To Robert Clark Jacob for 1 Black Horse 15 hands high
3 years old Imp. by Nicholas Currell by order of Col.
William Griffin in Octobr 1781   50 - 0 - 0
To Do for 1700lb Beef Imp. by Tim. Conner in June 1781   17 - 0 - 0
8 To Do for 40lb Bacon for the Prison Guards in Apr.1781
@ 8d   1 - 6 - 8
To Do for Ferriages for the Militia on their March to
Gloster in 1781   1 - 9 - 9
    69 -16 - 5

To John Wormeley for 1 Grey Horse 14½ hands high 6 years
old Imp. by George Guthrie in August 1781   55 - 0 - 0
117 To Do for Beef Imp. by Rawh Tapscott D. Com. for John
Brown in Octor 1781   8 -10 - 0
    63 -10 - 0

To Elias Edmonds for 1 Black Mare 14½ hands high 6 years
old Imp. by Nicholas Currell by order of Col. William
Griffin in Sept. 1781   36 - 0 - 0
104 To Do for Beef Imp. by Rawh Tapscott D. Com. for John
Brown in Octor 1781   5 - 0 - 0
    41 - 0 - 0

To Capt James Ewell for 1 Gun detained by General Weadon
at the Seige of York   3 - 0 - 0
77 To Do for Beef Imp. by Rawh Tapscott D. Com. Octor 81   5 -10 - 0
To Do for Boat Hire in carrying the Troops over Rappahk
River in March 1782   1 -10 - 0
To Do for Mutton & Lamb furnished the Guard in May & Sept.
1781   1 - 2 - 0
    11 - 2 - 0

To Nicholas George Commissary to the different Guards in Lancaster County in 1781	12 - 10 - 0
To D° for Necessarys furnished the said Guards	12 - 3 - 3
19 To D° for Beef Imp. by Raw^h Tapscott D. Com. in June 1781	9 - 16 - 6
To D° for 74¼ Gal. Brandy Rec^d by the Commissioners of the Tax in Oct°^r 1780	33 - 7 - 6
	67 - 17 - 3

To Jesse George D. Com. in Lancaster County d° for Beef No. 118 ₤2-5 in 1781	22 - 15 - 0

To Capt Robert Chinn for a Gun lost while on Duty at the Seige of York in 1781	3 - 0 - 0
No. 7 To D° for Beef Imp. by Raw^h Tapscott D. Com. June 1781	3 - 16 - 4
39 To D° d° d° July 1781	2 - 0 - 0
	8 - 16 - 4

To Job Carter, Goaler, for Imprisoning Deserters & Soldiers in 1781	8 - 7 - 0
To d° for keeping the County Magazine	4 - 0 - 0
	12 - 7 - 0

To the Est^t of Raw^h Downman Esqr dec^d for Beef Imp. by Raw^h Tapscott D. Com. June 1781	19 - 17 - 0
113 To D° for 1225 l^b Beef Imp. by Raw^h Tapscott D. C. in Octr 1781	12 - 5 - 0
To D° for 15 Gall. Brandy Imp. by Sam: Guthrie by order of Col. Taylor Sepr 1781	6 - 15 - 0
	38 - 17 - 0

30 To John Clayton for Beef Imp. by Raw^h Tapscott D. C. in June 1781	4 - 5 - 7
2 To Thomas Stott for d° d° May 1781	3 - 10 - 4
95 To John Miller for d° d° Oc^r 1781	2 - 15 - 0
21 To George Campbell d° d° June 1781	3 - 12 - 6
13 To Richd Goodridge d° d° June 1781	3 - 11 - 9
18 To Col. Edwin Conway for d° d° d°	7 - ₤ - 0
1 To D° d° d° May 1781	16 - 0 - 0
To d° for necessarys furnished the prison Guards in 1780 & 1781	3 - 19 - 4
	27 - 11 - 4

61 To Henry Lawson for Beef Imp. by Raw^h Tapscott D. C. July 1781	3 - 10 - 0
87 To Mary Lawson d° d° Oc^r 1781	3 - 10 - 0
To d° for 1 Gallon Brandy rec^d by Commissioners of the Tas Oc^r 1780	9
	3 - 19 - 0

88 To Henry Currell for Beef Imp. by Raw^h Tapscott D. C. Oc^r 1781	3 - 0 - 0

To d° for Lamb Imp. by Sam¹. Eddings Capt Art. Aug. 1781   0 - 18 - 0
                                                            3 - 18 - 0

52 To William Brent for Beef Imp. by Raw^h Tapscott D. C.
   July 1781   2 - 10 - 0
To d° for the use of his cart   Oc^r 1780   0 - 4 - 0
                                                            2 - 14 - 0

116 To James Wallace for Beef Imp. by Raw^h Tapscott D.C.
    Oc^r 1781   2 - 10 - 0
40 To Thomas Flint for d°   d°   July 1781   1 - 10 - 0
60 To Thomas Lawson   d°   d°   d°   3 - 10 - 0
    To d° for Necessarys furnished the Guards in Feb^r and
    March 1781   4 - 11 - 7
                                                            8 - 1 - 7

90 To Col. John Fleet for Beef Imp. by Raw^h Tapscott D.C.
   Octr 1781   10 - 10 - 0
   To d° for necessarys furnished the Guards   Novr 1780   1 - 19 - 7
                                                           12 - 9 - 7

98 To Eliz: Saunders for Beef Imp. by Raw^h Tapscott D.C.
   Octr 1781   3 - 0 - 0
96 To Thomas Hubbard   d°   d°   d°   2 - 10 - 0
54 To James Tapscott   d°   d°   July 1781   8 - 15 - 0
   To D° for Bacon furnished the Prison Guards Apr¹ /81   18
                                                            9 - 13 - 0

41 To Mungo Harvey for Beef Imp. by Raw^h Tapscott D.C.
   July 1781   5 - 0 - 0
N° 64 To Nicholas Currell for Beef Imp. by Raw^h
      Tapscott D. C. Octo^r 1781   6 - 0 - 0
   To D° for Necessarys furnished the Guards in June &
   Augt 1781   1 - 1 - 2
                                                            7 - 1 - 2

14 To the Es^t of Fortunatus Sydnor dec^d for Beef Imp.
   by Raw^h Tapscott June 1781   2 - 10 - 0
91 To William Griggs for d°   d°   Octr 1781   3 - 0 - 0
   To d° for Sundrys taken by Sam: Eddings, Capt Art.
   Aug. 1781   2 - 8 - 0
   To d° for Boy & Horses for   d°   0 - 5 - 0
                                                            5 - 13 - 0

23 To Joseph Shearman for Beef Imp. by Raw^h Tapscott
   D. C. June 1781   4 - 0 - 7
16 To Eliz: McTyre for   d°   d°   d°   3 - 0 - 0
63 To James Newby   d°   d°   Aug. 1781   4 - 0 - 0
   To John Chilton for Beef taken by Thos Walker June 1781 2 - 5 - 0
   To Robert Gilmoure for d° Imp. by Richd Eastin Novr 1781 5 - 8 - 5
   To d° for 603^lb Bacon for the use of the minute service
   under the command of Col. Peter P. Thornton in July
   1776 @ 7^d ½   18 -16 -16

	To D⁰ for 1 Dark Bay Horse 14 hands 12 y. old Imp. by Chaˢ Lee by Oʳ. his Excellency Thoˢ Nelson Ocʳ /81	20 - 0 - 0
81	To D⁰ for Beef Imp. by Rawʰ Tapscott D. Com. Ocʳ 1781	2 - 15 - 0
		47 - 0 - 3

	To Gawin Lowry for Ferriages over Corotoman River in 1781	5 - 7 - 2
29	To Elmore Doggett for Beef Imp. by Rawʰ Tapscott D. Com. June 1781	3 -10 - 0
51	To d⁰ d⁰ d⁰ July	2 -10 - 0
		6 - 0 - 0

38	To Mʳˢ Mary Tapscott for Pasturage for Beef Cattle by R. Tapscott June /81	5 - 0 - 0
10	To d⁰ Beef d⁰	4 - 0 - 0
116	To d⁰ d⁰ Ocʳ. /81	2 - 0 - 0
		11 - 0 - 5

25	To Edney Tapscott for Beef Imp. by R. Tapscott D. Com. June 1781	5 -18 - 6
36	To Matthew Myars d⁰ d⁰ d⁰	4 -12 - 4
	To d⁰ for 1 Mutton for the Guards July	0 -10 - 0
		5 - 2 - 4

37	To Thomas Myars d⁰ d⁰ d⁰	4 -12 - 4
	To d⁰ for 121½ˡᵇ Bacon & 1 Lamb for the Guards, June/81	4 - 7 - 0
		8 -19 - 4

74	To James Kirkes Est. for Beef Imp. by Rawʰ Tapscott D. C. Ocʳ 1781	3 -10 - 0
82	To Edward Carter d⁰ d⁰ d⁰	8 -10 - 0
	To d⁰ for 24 Gallons of Brandy Imp. by. P. Tillman by Oʳ. Col. John Taylor Sepᵗ /81	10 -16 - 0
		19 - 6 - 0

111	To William Brown for Beef Imp. by R. Tapscott D.C. Ocʳ 1781	3 -10 - 0
6	To Joseph Norris d⁰ d⁰ May 1781	1 -15 - 0
47	To William Yopp d⁰ d⁰ July	2 -15 - 0
83	To Sarah Bond d⁰ d⁰ Ocʳ	2 -15 - 0
50	To Jonathan Pullen d⁰ d⁰ July	2 -10 - 0
24	To Ann Shearman d⁰ d⁰ June	3 - 5 - 0
	To d⁰ for 1 Bus. Pease d⁰ for the Guards-March	0 - 4 - 0
		3 - 9 - 0

15	To William Carpenter for Beef Imp. by R. Tapscott D.C. June	3 - 9 - 0
46	To Joshua Hubbard d⁰ d⁰ July	3 - 0 - 0
N⁰ 100	To Col. James Gordon for Beef Imp. by Rawʰ Tapscott C. Com. Octoʳ 1781	£ 6 - 0 - 0
107	To Nathaniel Gordon d⁰ d⁰ d⁰	4 - 0 - 0
67	To George Norris d⁰ d⁰ d⁰	3 - 0 - 0
86	To Ann Stephens d⁰ d⁰ d⁰	2 -15 - 0
70	To the Est. of Charles Bell decᵈ d⁰ d⁰	4 - 0 - 0
56	To William Chilton d⁰ d⁰ July 1781	1 -16 - 0

69 To Coleman Doggett	d^o	d^o	Oc^r	3 - 0 - 0	
97 To William Schofield	d^o	d^o	d^o	3 - 0 - 0	
To D^o for 7½ Gall. Brandy Rec^d by Comms. of the Tax Oc^r 1780				3 - 7 - 6	
				6 - 7 - 6	

109 To John Carter for Beef Imp. by R. Tapscott D. Com. Oc^r 1781 — 3 - 0 - 0
To D^o for 6^{lb} Bacon furnished prison Guards Oc^r /80 — 4
To Judith Yerby for Beef Imp. by R. Tapscott D. Comm. July — 3 - 0 - 0

108 To Stephen Chilton	d^o	d^o	Oc^r	3 - 0 - 0
76 To John Davis	d^o	d^o	d^o	2 -10 - 0
85 To John Cundiff	d^o	d^o	d^o	2 -10 - 0
110 To John Bean	d^o	d^o	d^o	3 - 0 - 0
105 To William Edwards	d^o	d^o	d^o	3 - 5 - 0
106 To Joseph Dobbs	d^o	d^o	d^o	2 -10 - 0
75 To Elizabeth Hill	d^o	d^o	d^o	3 - 5 - 0
84 To Harry Carter	d^o	d^o	d^o	3 - 0 - 0
68 To Abner Palmer	d^o	d^o	d^o	3 - 0 - 0
71 To Thomas Robb	d^o	d^o	d^o	2 - 5 - 0
101 To Jedithen Pinckard	d^o	d^o	d^o	2 -10 - 0
73 To Ellen Lizenby	d^o	d^o	d^o	2 - 0 - 0
3 To William Stott	d^o	d^o	May 1781	4 - 5 - 4
To D^o for 106^{lb} Bacon	d^o	d^o	@ 8^d	3 -10 - 8
				7 -16 - 0

9 To William Sydnor for Beef Imp. by R. Tapscott D.C. June — 10 -17 - 2
To D^o for a Mutton furnished the Guards July — 10
To D^o for 20 Gallons Brandy & Cask Imp. by Henry Pointer by order of Col. John Taylor @ 9/ Sepr 1781 — 9 - 3 - 0
— 20 -10 - 2

11 To Moore Fauntleroy for Beef Imp. by R. Tapscott D.C. June — 2 -19 - 0

42 To D^o	d^o	d^o	July	3 - 5 - 0
				6 - 4 - 0
65 To Jonathan Wilder	d^o	d^o	Oc^r	3 - 5 - 0
12 To William Warren	d^o	d^o	June	3 -19 - 0
44 To D^o	d^o	d^o	July	2 -10 - 0
				6 - 9 - 0
78 To William Wiblin	d^o	d^o	Oc^r	1 -10 - 0
62 To Mrs Alice Smith	d^o	d^o	July	11 -15 - 0

No 80 To Mrs Agatha Ball for Beef Imp. by Raw^h Tapscott D. Com. Oc^r 1781 — 7 - 0 - 0
To D^o for Corn furnished the Troops on their March to York in September 1781 — 0 - 8 - 0
— 7 - 8 - 0

115	To Charles Rogers for Beef Imp. by R. Tapscott D. C. Oc^r				3-15 - 0
17	To D^o	d^o	d^o	June	3 - 0 - 2
	To D^o for Beef & Mutton furnished the Guards in Feby 1781				1 - 7 - 0
					8 - 2 - 2

55	To James Simmonds for Beef Imp. by R. Tapscott D.C.			July	3 -10 - 0
72	To Thomas Robb	d^o	d^o	Oc^r	2 -10 - 0
48	To Benjamin George	d^o	d^o	July	3 - 0 - 0
49	To Mary Haydon	d^o	d^o	d^o	2 - 0 - 0
32	To William Martin	d^o	d^o	June	3 - 0 - 0
31	To Thomas Carter	d^o	d^o	d^o	2 - 5 - 0
	To d^o for Necessarys furnished the Guards Novr 1780				3 - 6 - 0
					5 -11 - 0

99	To James Pinckard	d^o	d^o	Oc^r "	3 - 0 - 0
58	To William Chowning	d^o	d^o	July	4 -16 - 0
	To D^o for 30 Gall. Brandy Rec^d by Comms. of Tax Octo^r 1780				13 -10 - 0
					18 - 6 - 0

66	To John Harris for Beef Imp. by R. Tapscott D.C. Oc^r 1781				3 -15 - 0
59	To John Chowning	d^o	d^o	July	2 - 0 - 0
	To D^o for Ferriages &c. on Rappah^k in Sept^r & Oc^{t}o^r 1781				43 -15 - 0
					45 -15 - 0

92	To Henry Hinton for Beef Imp. by R. Tapscott D. C. Oc^r 1781				2 -10 - 0
94	To James Brent	d^o	d^o	d^o	2 -10 - 0
	To D^o for Necessarys furnished the Guards in 1781				2 - 1 - 0
					4 -11 -10

34	To Thoman Hunton for Beef Imp. by Raw^h Tapscott D.C. June 1781				6 -15 - 0
	To D^o for Necessarys furnished the Guards			Aug.	1 -14 - 0
	To d^o	d^o	d^o	July	4 - 7 - 7
					12 -16 - 7

33	To John Berryman for Beef Imp. by Raw^h Tapscott D.C. June 1781				8 - 0 - 0
	To d^o for provisions furnished the Guards			July	1 - 4 - 0
					9 - 4 - 0

22	To William Dunaway for Beef Imp. by Raw^h Tapscott D.C. June				3 - 5 - 0
26	To John Longwith	d^o	d^o	d^o	4 - 5 - 0
	To John Roberts for 301^{lb} Salted Beef furnished the Guards Mar. 1781 3^d				3 -15 - 3
	To D^o for 314½^{lb}	d^o	d^o	Feb^r 3^d	3-18- 7½
					7-13-10½

	To William Merrideth for Stalling two Beaves		July 1781	0 - 6 - 0
	To d^o for Mutton furnished the Guards		Aug.	0 -10 - 0
				0 -16 - 0

To Samuel Yopp for 30 Gall.Brandy Imp. by Paul Tilman by
order of Col. John Taylor in Septr 1781 @ 9/   13-13 - 0
To William Doggett for 286^{lb} Bacon furnished the Guards
June 1781 @ 8^d 9 -10 -18
To James Flemming for Pork for   d^o July   0 -10 - 0
To Jemima Blakemore for Necessarys furnished the Guards in
June 1781   £ 1 - 4 - 9
To Elijah Percifull for certain services by order of the
Comanding Officer in 1781   0 -10 - 0
To William Boatman for Necessarys furnished the Guards in
Novr 1780   0 - 9 - 0
To Henry Towles for 24 Gall^s Brandy Imp. by Saml Guthrie by
or. Col. Jno Taylor Sep^r_d/81   10 -16 - 0
To d^o for 20 Barl^s Corn rec^d by Commissioners of the Tax
Octr 1780   10 - 0 - 0
To d^o for Sundries furnished the Guards   June 1781   1 - 2 - 6
    21 -18 - 6

To Andrew Robertson for 27$\frac{1}{4}$ Gall^s Brandy rec^d by Commiss^{rs}
of Tax in Oc^r 1780   12 - 5 - 3
To Thomas Lee for 562 Gall^s Rum and Brandy Rec^d by D^o 252 -18 - 0
To John Tarpley for a Pilote 7 Days --- by Richd Taylor
Octr 1781   2 - 0 - 0
To John Eustace for Sundrys furnished the Guards   d^o 10 -11 - 3
To d^o d^o d^o Apr^l 0 -18 - 9
To Judith Brent for Necessarys furnished d^o in July 1781   1 - 7 - 0
N° 93 To   d^o for Beef Imp. by Raw^h Tapscott D. Comm. Oc^r 3 - 0 - 0
28 To D^o d^o d^o July   2 -15 - 0
    7 - 2 - 0

To Col. James Ball for 86$\frac{1}{2}$^{lb} Bacon for the use of the Army
June 1781   2 -17 - 8
114 To Dr William Ball for Beef Imp. by R. Tapscott D.C.
Oc^r 6 - 0 - 0
103 To Thad^s McCarty   d^o d^o d^o 3 - 0 - 0
To D^o for necessarys furnished the Guards   Aug. 1780   5 - 0 - 0
    8 - 0 - 0

43 To Mrs Margaret Ball for Beef Imp. by R. Tapscott D.C.
July 1781   3 -15 - 0
To Edwd Blakemore for removing 6 hh^d publick Tob^o from the
Warehouse by order of the Commissioners of the Tax in 1781
    1 - 4 - 0
79 To Jesse Chilton for Beef Imp. by R. Tapscott D. Com.
Oc^r /81   3 -15 - 0"
19 April 1782 - p. 95 et seq.

    "It is ordered to be Certified by the Clerk of this Court to the
Auditors of Publick Accounts that H. Towles and H. Lawson Gent: the
Commissioners of the Grain Tax in this County in the year 1781, are
allowed the sum of Three pounds @ for their services therein" 16
May 1782 - p. 99

14

It appearing to the Court that John Taylor Gent: late Sheriff of the said County of Lancaster had Credited sundry persons Inhabitants thereof with Commissioners Certificates for Brandy &c. for the use of the Army agreeable to an Act of the General Assembly in that case made and provided, and that the said Taylor hath not hitherto been allowed in any settlement with the Auditors of Public Accounts for the said Brandy &c., the same are allowed as Just Claims as followeth:

£

To William Carpenter for 3 Gal. & 3 Qt^s Brandy rec^d by Common^{rs}
of the Tax in October 1780 @ 9/   1-13 - 9
To William Stott for 2 G. & 3 Qt^s d^o 1- 4 - 9
To Spencer Brown for 2 Qt^s $\frac{1}{2}$ Pt do   6 - 5$\frac{1}{2}$
To Joseph Wilkerson for 2 Qt^s d^o 4 - 6
To Jesse Robinson for 1 G. 3 Q. 1 p^t d^o 16 -10$\frac{1}{2}$
To Bushrod Riveer for 2 G. 3 Q^t d^o 1- 4 - 9
To John Riveer for 2 Qt^s d^o 4 - 6
To Thomas Dunaway for 1 G. & 1 p^t d^o 10 - 1$\frac{1}{2}$
To Thomas Pitman for 1 G. 3 Qt^s 1 Pt d^o 16 -10$\frac{1}{2}$
To the Rever^d John Leland for 3 G. 2 Qt^s d^o 1-11 - 6
To Henry Tapscott's Est for 9 G. 3$\frac{1}{2}$ Qt^s d^o 4-10
To Richd Mitchell for 2 G. & 1 p^t d^o 19 -1$\frac{1}{2}$
To Richd Ball for 7 g. 3 Q^t & 1 p^t d^o 3-10 -10$\frac{1}{2}$
To George Cammell for 1 G. 3 Qt^s d^o 15 - 9
To Richd Goodridge for 3 G. 3 Q^t 1 p^t d^o 1-14 - 3
To Richd Cundiff for 4$\frac{1}{2}$ Gall^{ns} d^o 2-   6
To John Boyd for $\frac{1}{2}$ Gall^n d^o 4 - 6
To James Riveer for 1 Gall^n d^o 9
To William Riveer Ju^r for 1 d^o d^o 9
To Robert Chinn for 8 Gal^n d^o 3-12 -
To John Chilton for 3 Qt^s d^o 6 - 9
To Ozwals Newby for 4 Gal^{ns} d^o 1-16 -
To Jesse Robinson Ju^r for 1$\frac{1}{2}$ Gall^{ns} d^o 13 - 6
To William Montague for 16$\frac{1}{2}$ Gal^{ns} d^o 7- 8 - 8$\frac{1}{2}$
To Stephen Lock for 3 G. 1 1/3 p^t d^o 1- 8 -11$\frac{1}{4}$
To Col. Edwin Conway for 63 Gal^{ns} d^o 28- 7 -
To James Newby for 5 G. 2 Q^t 1 p^t d^o 2-10 -10$\frac{1}{2}$
To James Norris for 2$\frac{1}{2}$ Gal^{ns} d^o 19 - 1
To Peter Conway for 6 G. 2$\frac{1}{2}$ Qt^s d^o 2-19 -7$\frac{1}{4}$
To Col. James Ball for 50 G.   d^o 22-10 -
To Col. James Gordon for 44 G. 1$\frac{1}{2}$ p^t Brandy   £   19-17 - 4
To Thomas Carter for 3 G. 2$\frac{1}{2}$ Qt^s d^o 1-15 - 2
To Maurice Wheeler for 1 Gal^n d^o 9
To Newton Brent for 3 Gal^{ns} d^o 1- 7
To Elizabeth James for 2 Gal^n d^o 18
To Bailie George for 3 Gal^n d^o 1- 7
To Thomas Hunton for 7$\frac{1}{2}$ Gal^{ns} d^o 3- 7 - 6
To Betty Saunders for 2 G. 1$\frac{1}{2}$ p^t d^o 19 -1$\frac{1}{2}$
To John Merideth for 7 Gal^n d^o 3- 3 -
To Joseph Hubbard for 1 G. 2$\frac{1}{2}$ Qt^s d^c 15 - 5
To William Stephens for 2 G. 2$\frac{1}{2}$ Qt^s d^o 1- 3 -7$\frac{1}{2}$
To James Pollard for 1$\frac{1}{2}$ Gall^n d^o 15 - 6
To John Berryman for 10 Gal^n 1 Q^t d^o 4-12 - 1

To John Parrott for 3 G. $2\frac{1}{2}$ Qt^s d^o	1 - 12 - 6
To Henry Lawson for 9 Gal^n 2 Qt^t $1\frac{1}{2}$ p^t d^o	4 - 7 - $5\frac{1}{2}$
To Mary Lawson for 5 G. $3\frac{1}{2}$ Qt^s d^o	1 - 15 - $1\frac{1}{4}$
To John Davis for 2 Gal^{ns} d^c	18
To Henry Currell for $8\frac{7}{8}$ Gal^{ns} d^o	3 - 16 - 6
To Isaac Currell for $2\frac{1}{4}$ Gal^n $\frac{1}{2}$ p^t d^o	1 - 4 - 9
To Thomas Lawson for 9 1/8 Gal^n d^o	4 - 1 - $3\frac{1}{4}$
To William Mitchell for 5 G. 2 Qt^s $\frac{1}{2}$ p^t d^o	2 - 10 -
To Charles Lee for 8 G. $1\frac{1}{2}$ p^t d^c	3 - 13 - $11\frac{1}{2}$
To Eleazer Robinson for $1\frac{1}{2}$ G. d^c	13 - 6
To Isaac Degge for 4 Gal. & $\frac{1}{2}$ p^t d^c	1 - 16 - 10
To John McTyre for 8 d^o d^c	3 - 12 -
To Nicholas Currell for 7 G. $1\frac{1}{4}$ p^t d^o	3 - 4 - $4\frac{3}{4}$
To Elizabeth McTyre for 5 d^o d^c	2 - 5 -
To James Currell Ju^r for $1\frac{3}{4}$ Gal^{ns} d^c	15 - 9
To Raw^h Downman's Es^t. for 33 d^o & $\frac{1}{4}$ p^t d^o	15 - 5 - 8
To James Currell for 1 G. $3\frac{1}{2}$ Qt^s d^c	16 - $10\frac{1}{4}$
To John Chinn for 29 G. 3 Qt^s & $\frac{1}{4}$ p^t d^c	13 - 8 - 10
To Thomas Pinckard for 28 G. & $\frac{1}{2}$ p^t d^o	12 - 12 - 6
To Judith Brent for $8\frac{3}{4}$ Bu^s Salt @	
To William Griggs for 7 Gal^s d^o	5 - 3 -
To John & Thos Carter for $47\frac{11}{11}$lb Bacon @ 8^d	1 - 11 - 2
To Martin George for 3 G. $1\frac{1}{2}$ p^t d^c	1 - 8 - $2\frac{1}{4}$
To Mrs Alice Smith for 17 Barl^s 2 Bu^s Corn @ 10/	8 - 12 -
To William Mason for 3 G. 3 Qt^s $1\frac{1}{2}$ p^t d^c	1 - 3 - $0\frac{1}{4}$
To Charles Bell for 8 Bu^s $2\frac{1}{2}$ Pecks Salt @	
To Eliz^a James Ju^r for 2 Gal^n d^o	18
To James Brent for $7\frac{1}{2}$ Bu^s Salt @	
To John Longwith for $2\frac{1}{4}$ Gal^n d^o	1 - 2 - 6
To George Norris for $6\frac{1}{2}$ Bu^s Salt @	
To Judith Yerby for 4 Gal^s d^o	1 - 16 -
To William Gibson for 2 G. 3 Qt^s $\frac{1}{2}$ p^t d^c	1 - 15 - $3\frac{1}{2}$
To John Naughton for $3\frac{1}{2}$ Qt^s d^o	6 - $10\frac{1}{2}$
To Sarah James for 1 1/8 Gal^n d^c	9 - $1\frac{1}{2}$
To James Simmonds for 4 G. $3\frac{1}{2}$ Qt^s d^c	2 - 4 - $1\frac{1}{4}$
To John Clayton for 2 Gal^s d^c	18
To Harry Hinton for 9 Gal^{ns} d^c	4 - 1
To John James for 3 Gal^{ns} & 1 p^t d^o	1 - 8 - $1\frac{1}{2}$
To Fortunatus Sydnor for 6 G. 3 Q. 1 2/3 p^t d^c	3 - 2 - $4\frac{1}{2}$
To Joseph Dobbs for 2 G. $12\frac{1}{2}$ p^t d^o	1 - 0 - $4\frac{1}{2}$
To James Wallace for 3 Qt^s $1\frac{1}{2}$ p^t d^o	8 - $5\frac{1}{2}$
To Isaac Currell for $\frac{1}{2}$ pt do	$6\frac{1}{2}$
To Col. John Taylor for 29 G. 2 Qt^s $\frac{1}{4}$ p^t d^o	13 - 6 - $7\frac{1}{2}$
To William Schofield for 1 G. 2 Qt^s $\frac{1}{4}$ p^t d^o	14 - 4
To George Carter for 4 G. 1 Q^t $\frac{1}{2}$ p^t d^c	1 - 18 - 3
To William Doggett for 3 Gal^{ns} d^c	1 - 7 -
To Thomas Brent for 4 Gal^s $\frac{1}{2}$ p^t d^o	1 - 16 - 6
To William Brown for 4 Gal^s d^o	1 - 16 -
To William Kirk for $2\frac{1}{3}$ Gal d^o	1 - 2 - 6
To William Lawson for $3\frac{1}{2}$ d^c	1 - 11 - 6
To Elijah Percifull for $1\frac{1}{4}$ d^c	11 - 3
To John Flowers for 5 d^o d^o	2 - 5 -
To Charles Williams for 1 G. & $\frac{1}{4}$ p^t d^o	9 - 6

16

To Elijah Robinson for 3 G. 1 Q^t 1 p^t	d^o	1 - 10 - 11	
To Coleman Doggett for 6 1/8 Gal^n	do	2 - 15 - $\frac{1}{2}$	
To Edny Tepscott for 6$\frac{1}{2}$ d^o	d^o	2 - 16 - 3	
To John Miller for 2$\frac{3}{4}$ d^o	d^o	1 - 4 - 9	
To Betty Hill for 3 d^c	d^o	1 - 7 -	
To Lawson Hathaway for 9 G. 3$\frac{1}{2}$ Q^t do	d^o	4 - 8 -10$\frac{1}{2}$	
To Thomas Hathaway for 3 G. 3$\frac{1}{2}$ Q^{ts}	d^o	1 - 14 - 11	
To William George for 2$\frac{1}{4}$ Q^{ts}	do	5 - 0	
To Jesse George for 2$\frac{1}{2}$ Gal^s	d^o	1 - 2 - 6	
To Job Carter for 8 d^o	d^o	3 - 12 -	
To Abner Palmer for 2 G. & $\frac{1}{2}$ p^t	d^o	18 - 6	
To Mary & Richd Selden for 19 G. 3 l. $\frac{1}{2}$ p^t	d^o	8 - 18 - 3$\frac{1}{2}$	
To John Selden for 6 1/8 G.	d^o	2 - 14 - 1$\frac{1}{2}$	
To Rodham Lunsford for 10 Gal^s	d^o	4 - 10 -	
To Willoughby Rout for 1 G. 1$\frac{1}{4}$ p^t	d^o	11 - 1	
To John Sebrie for 1 1/8 G.	d^o	10 - 1$\frac{1}{2}$	
To Robert Belvaird for 2 G. 1$\frac{1}{2}$ d^c		1 - 1 - 4$\frac{1}{2}$	
To Presly Neale for 3 Q^{ts} 1$\frac{1}{2}$ d^o		8 - 5$\frac{1}{2}$	
To William Bean for 1$\frac{1}{2}$ Q^t	d^c	- 2 - 6	
To Peter Riveer for 1 Gal^n	d^o	9	
To John Payne for 3 G. 2 Q^{ts}	d^o	1 - 4 - 6	
To William Warren for 7 G. 3 Q^{ts} $\frac{1}{2}$ p^t	d^o	3 - 10 - 3	
To Joseph Stephens for 4$\frac{1}{2}$ Gal	d^c	2 - - 6	
To Eliz^a Biscoe for 3$\frac{1}{2}$ d^c	d^c	1 - 11 - 6	
To John Bailey for 4 d^o	d^c	1 - 16 -	
To Nicholas George for 8 G. 1 Q^t 2/3 p^t	d^o	3 - 15 - 1	
To James Ewell for 15 G.	d^o	6 - 15 -	
To Edward Carter for 14 G. 1$\frac{1}{2}$ Q^t	d^c	6 - 9 - 1$\frac{1}{2}$	
To William Sydnor for 22 G. 2$\frac{1}{2}$ Q^{ts}	d^o	10 - 3 - 7$\frac{1}{2}$	
To James Pullen for 2$\frac{1}{2}$ Q^{ts}	d^o	5 - 7$\frac{1}{2}$	
To Doct^r Andrew Robertson for 12 G. 3$\frac{1}{2}$ Q^{ts}	d^c	5 - 15 - 4	
To Thomas Flint for 3 G.	d^o	1 - 7 -	
To Johnson Riveer for 5 1/8 G.	d^o	2 - 6 - 1$\frac{1}{2}$	
To Joseph Norris for 4$\frac{3}{4}$ G.	d^o	2 - 2 - 9	
To John Norris for 2 G. 2$\frac{1}{2}$ Q^{ts}	d^o	1 - 3 - 7$\frac{1}{2}$	
To Peter Conway for 22 G. 1$\frac{1}{4}$ Q^{ts}	d^c	10 - - 9	
To Joseph Goodridge for 3 G. 3$\frac{1}{2}$ Q^{ts}	d^o	1 - 14 -10	
		£394 - 10 - 8	

Also
To John Taylor Gent: for Sundries as p^r Rec^t from Thos Boulware and
Thomas Wood Gent: Commissioners of Essex County, to-wit:

for 4238^{lb} Superfine Flower @ 18/ p^r $\cancel{c}^t$ July 1780		£38 - 2 - 0
1336^{lb} Brown Biscuit @ 18/ p^r c^t	d^c	12 - 0 - 5
32 Caskes @ 2/	d^o	3 - 4 - 0
6 Bushels Pease @ 4/	d^c	12 - 0 - 0
N° 75 To James Brown, assigned to John Taylor)		
for 1525^{lb} Beef Imp. by John McWilliams) Aug.1781		13 - 5 - 0
Comm^r @ 20/ p^r c^t	)£394-10-8	
		78 -11 - 5

4 To the Est^t of Richd Mitchell Gent: dec^d for)
300^{lb} Beef Imp. by Raw^h Tapscott D. Com.) May 1781
for John Brown @ 20/)   3 - 0 - 0

To d° for Stalling s^d Beef	7 - 6
8 To d° for 675^lb Beef Imp. by d° @ 20/ June 1781	6 - 15 - 0
To d° for Stalling s^d Beef	0 - 15 - 0
To d° for 1 Tunn hh^d and Cart & Driver two Days by Saml Guthrie by order of Col. John Taylor Sepr 1781	1 - 2 - 0
	11 - 19 - 6
To Charles Carter Esqr Assigned to Matthew Myers for 4259^lb Beef Imp. by Thos Garland C.P.L. Hanover County Novemb^r 1780	42 - 11 - 6
To Nathaniel Burwell Esqr for Sundries as p^r Certificates & Orders in 1780, to-wit: 50 & ½ Barl^s Indian Corn @ 10/ £25-5-0 ---- to Ano^t £2-3-9	27 - 8 - 9
To Joseph Dobbs, Armourer, to the 4th Reg^t. Militia Octo^r 1781	12 - 0 - 0
To James Gordon for 1 Bay Horse 11 y^rs old 14½ hands high Imp. by N. Currell by O^r of Col. W. Griffin	20 - 0 - 0
To Joseph Shearman for Horse & Tumbler three days	1 - 0 - 0
To John Webb for carrying Clothing for the Soldiers to Fred'burg	2 - 16 - 0"

21 June, 1782 - p. 103 et seq.

"One Bay Horse 14½ hands high Eleven Years old Impressed by Nicholas Currell by order of Col. William Griffin belonging to Col. James Gordon valued by the Court at £20 which is ordered to be Certified to the next Assembly" 17 Oct. 1782 - p. 117

"The following Certificates were received by the Court as just Claims against the publick, and are ordered to be Certified, to-wit:
Thad^s McCarty as p^r Certificate from Richd Young for Freight of Brandy £ 75 - 0 - 0
To James Tapscott for Beef Imp. by R. Tapscott D. C. for J. Brown 3 - 15 - 0" 16 Jan. 1783 - p. 124

"The Sheriff of this County is ordered to give public notice to all persons within the said County who has sustained any loss by the depredations of the Enemy to attend on the second day of March Court next with a perfect and proper Account of the same as also what proof can be had in justification thereof" 20 Feb. 1783 - p.126

At a Special Court held at Lancaster Courthouse the 17th day of April 1783, Pursuant to an Act of the General Assembly for Ascertaining the losses & Injuries sustained from the Depredations of the Enemy within this Com.Wealth.

Present James Ball & others - Six members.

To Mingo Harvey for 2 Negroes Will & Kitt) proved by his own oath)	220 - -	
To John Payne for one Negro James proved by his own oath	100 - -	
To John Selden for one D⁰ Daniel Butler Proved by his own oath	100 - -	
	420 - -	

Signed by Ja^S Ball

And At a Court held the 16th of May following in pursuance of the afores^d Act of Assembly -

Present James Ball &c. - Six members

To John Eustace for a Quantity of Household Furniture, Cloathing, Beding, Table furniture also a Quant. of Cash and Plate - To the amount of it lost	253 - -
Also 5 Negro Men from 20 to 26 years of Age valued at	550 - -
	803 - -

Transmitted.   Signed by Ja^S Ball.

p. 128

"At a Special Court held at Lancaster Courthouse the 21st Day of March 1783 Pursuant to an Act of the General Assembly Intitled An Act to Ascertain the losses and Injuries sustained from the Depredations of the Enemy within this Common Wealth

Present   (James Ball   William Yorby)
                (Henry Towles   Henry Lawson   ) Gent: Justices
                (John Fleet   James Tapscott)

Mary Lawson:
     1 Negro Man Joshua, proved by the Oath of
Henry Lawson   £ 100 - " -

George Currell:
     One Negro Man, Oliver, proved by the Oath of
Henry Lawson   100 -

Rawleigh Shearman:
     One Negro Man, James, proved by the Oath of Henry
Lawson   100 -

Thomas Hunton:
     Two Negroes, Jack & Daniel, proved by John Fleet &
Hen: Lawson   220 -

William Martin:
     One Negro Abraham, proved by the Oath of Thomas
Carter   120 -

John Fleet:
     Two Negroes, Ambrose & Willoughby, proved by
Thomas Hunton   240 -

Jemima Blakemore:
    One Negro man Will, proved by Jonathan Denison 100 –

Rodham Lunsford:
    One negro man Moses   £120 –
    38 Barl^s Tar £38 – A Cable &c including the)
Damages his Vessel Sustained £ 62 – Proved by his own oath)
                                          100 –   ) 220 –

Joseph Carter dec. Est:
    Two Negroes Angulus & Tom £100 & 70 – , proved
by Rod^m Lunsford   170 –

Isaac Degge:
    Three Negroes, Spencer, Solomon & Tom £ 120 – 100 –
& 100 – Proved by Thos Carter   320 –

William Hinton:
    16 Salt Kettles @ 25/ cash, proved by Thomas
Hinton   20 –

Thomas Myars:
    One Negro Man, Dennis, proved by Matthew Myars   120 –
                                                                           £ 1830 –

                                                                             1830 –

Matthew Myars:
    One Negro, Dick £120, 42 Bu^s Salt £31-10 & 1
Petty Auger £6 – Proved by his own oath   157-10-0

Thomas Carter:
    One Petty Auger – proved by his own oath   2- 5-

George Yerby:
    One Negro man, Nace, proved by Eppa Stott   100-

John Longwith:
    One Negro man, Ben, proved by his own oath   100-

Charles Carter, Esqr:
    16 Negroes, vizt John £100, Abraham 110, Alexander)
100, Billy 100, Lewis 100, Young 50, Tom 70, Daniel 70,)
Liah 70, Billy 80, Ben 50, Talbut 120, James 70, Adam)
100, Daniel 100, David 50, £1340 – 26 head of Sheep @)
12/ £ 15-12, A Bed & Furniture £ 12   27-12   ) 1367-12 –

Two Negroes Sam & Will £ 100 & 120   £220   )
Sundry Cloathing & Household furniture to Amo^t 38   )
Two hhd^s Tob^o 1857^{lb} Nett @ 20/ p^r C^t 18-10-10) 276-10-10
proved by his own oath.

Richard Selden:
    Two hhd^s Tob^o 1207 & 1120^{lb} Nett @ 20/ proved
by Wm Pitman   23- 5- 6

James Tapscott:
    Seven hhd^s Tob^o 7000^{lb} Nett @ 20/   £70)
    the half of a Sloop   100)
Three Negroes, Aaron £120, Isaac 100, Humphry   )
100   320)   495 -
a quantity of Paint, Rum hhd^s &c. to Amo^t 5)
Proved by his own oath

Elmore Doggett:
    One Negro Man, Dick, proved by Thomas Pollard   100 -

George Brent:
    one Schooner Boat, proved by his own Oath   200 -

Robert C. Jacob:
    Fourteen hhd^s Tob^o about 15000^{lb} Nett @ 20/   150 -
Proved by G. Brent.

James Brent:
    One Negro, Meshack, £120, Two Gunns £ 4, Sundry
Hogs &c. £ 2   126 -
    4924-2-10

£   4924-2-10

Judith George:
    Cash £ 4, Gun & Sword £ 10, House furniture &
wearing apparel £ 5, proved by her own Oath   29-"-"

William Chowning:
    Two Huns £ 6, one Musquet belonging to the public
£ 5, proved by his own Oath   11-

Thomas Ingram:
    One Gun £ 5, Sundry Cloaths &c. £ 10, proved by
his own Oath   15-

Mrs Alice Smith:
    Six Negroes, Viz^t: Tom £100, Jo 100, Grimes 80,)
Sarah 100 and two small negroes 60, proved by John   )   440-
Bailey.

Charles Lee:
    One Negro, Daniel, a valuable Pilate 200 £ &
Pilote Boat 200 £, proved by Richard Lee   400-"-"

Mrs Elizabeth Beale:
    One Negro Man, Jo, £100, A Wench & child £100,
proved by Richard Lee   200-

Robert Gilmour, dec^d Es^t:
    Two Negroes Moses & James, to the knowledge of
the Court   300-

Doct.^r William Ball:
 Three Negroes, Frank £ 100, Will 80, Tom 80, proved
by Henry Towles   260-

Thomas Pollard:
 The Foursail and Halliards of a Sloop, proved by
his own Oath   15-
                            Whole amount   £6594-2-10

 This Court is Dissolved & Sign'd by
                                    Ja.^s Ball
Transmitted. "
p. 128 et seq.

Orders 1783 to 1786 (17)

"The following Certificates were received by the Court as just Claims against the Publick, agreeable to an Act of Assembly, which were ordered to be Certified, vizt:

£

No 8 To Thad.^s McCarty and Assigned to Charles Mc Carty for
Freight of Brandy, Rum & Salt from the Commissioners of
the Tax Nov. 13th 1780   805-10-0
To d.^o for the same services Decr 16th 1780   384-10-0
27 To Thomas Pollard for Beef Imp. by Raw.^h Tapscott
D. C. June 25th 1781   5- 0-0 "
20 Mar. 1783 - p. 2

 "The Court then proceeded to Receive the following Certificates according to Law, vizt: N.º 111 To William Brown Imp.^d by Raw.^h Tapscott D. Com. 350^lb Beef Octo.^r 1781 £3-10-0

 Col. John Fleet's & Elijah Percifull's Certificates Transmitted" 16 May 1783 - p. 10

 "The Court then received a Claim against the Public of Nicholas George's agreeable to an Act of Assembly in that case made and provided, which is ordered to be Certified and is as followeth, vizt:
 To Nicholas George as Commissary to the Stationed Guards at Chownings & Towles's Point one Months Service   £ 3 - 0 - 0"
21 Aug. 1783 - p. 24

 "It is ordered to be Certified that William Newby Bailey is Heir at Law to Edward Bailey, dec.^d who was in the service of this State and since dead" 21 Aug. 1783 - p. 24

 "It is ordered to be Certified that John Newby is heir at Law to LeRoy Newby, dec.^d who was in the service of this State and since dead" 22 Aug. 1783 - p. 26

"It is ordered that the Clerk of this County Certify it to the Auditors of this State that Nancy Dye is the heir at Law to Jonathan Dye who died in the Continental Service at the Battle of German Town" 18 Sept. 1783 - p. 33

"Ordered the Clerk of this Court Certify to the Auditors of public Accounts that William Dunaway is Heir at Law to John Dunaway who died in the Regular Service.

Ordered the Clerk of this Court Certify to the Auditors of publick Accounts that Tarpley Thomas is Heir at Law to Amos Thomas who died in the Regular service.

Ordered the Clerk of this Court Certify to the Auditors of publick Accounts that Esther Wiblin is Heir at Law of the whole Blood to William Wiblin who died in the Regular service" 16 Dec. 1784 - p. 85

"Ordered to be Certified to the Auditors of Public Accounts that Sarah Ann Dye is the wife of Jonathan Dye a Lieutenant in the Continental Army who was killed in the Battle of German Town" 19 Aug. 1785 - p. 121

"Jane Burn a Pensioner and resident in this County has two small children and no support, the same is ordered to be Certified" 15 Dec. 1785 - p. 129

"George Pitman, a Pensioner and resident in this County has a wife & child and is possessed of a Negro wench and her child, is deprived of one of his legs which was lost in the Battle of Charles Town, South Carolina, the same is ordered to be Certified" 15 Dec. 1785 - p. 129

Orders 1786 to 1789 (18)

"Ordered to be Certified to the Auditors of Public Accounts that Leannah Overstreet is the widow of John Overstreet who died in the Navy service of this State, and that she has several small children and no support.

Ordered it be certified to the Auditors of Public Accounts that John Brent is the Heir of Richard Brent dec^d who died in the Navy Service of this State.

23

Ordered if be certified to the Auditors of Public Accounts that Aaron Dameron and James Davis intermarried with Ann and Elizabeth Perkins who are the heirs of Thomas & James Perkins that served in the Navy of this State, after went to Sea and has been absent about Eight years.

Ordered it be Certified to the Auditors of Public Accounts that John Newby is Heir to George and W^{m}son Newby who died in the Continental Service" 16 Feb. 1786 - p. 2

It is ordered to be further certified that Leannah Overstreet the widow of John Overstreet, who was an Inhabitant of Lancaster County and who died in the Revenge Gally belonging to the Navy of this State, about Thirty years of Age, has several small children and no support.

Ordered it be Certified to the Auditors of Public Accounts that Hannah Thatcher is the widow of William Thatcher, an inhabitant of Lancaster County & who died in the Revenge Gally belonging to the Navy of this State, about Twenty four years of Age, has several small children and no support.

Ordered it be certified to the Auditors of Public Accounts that Rachel Crowder was the widow of Martin Hill, an inhabitant of Lancaster County & who died in the Ship Dragon belonging to the Navy of this State about thirty two years of Age, and remained his widow until the 8th of June 1780, when she intermarried with Joshua Crowder, has several small children and no support.

Ordered it be Certified to the Auditors of Public Accounts that Isabel Dountain was the widow of Jesse Kent who was an inhabitant of Lancaster County & died as a Midshipman in the Revenge Gally belonging to the Navy of this State about Twenty seven years of age, and remained his widow until the 5th of June 1780, when she intermarried with William Dountain, has several small children and no support" 16 Mar. 1786 - p. 4

"Ordered to be Certified to the Auditors of Public Accounts that Nancy Jones is the widow of Lewis Jones the younger who served as a Masters Mate and Master on board of the Page Gally under the command of Capt James Markham from the 17th of June 1776 to the 28th of October 1779 agreeable to a certificate from under the said Markham's hand, and that the said Jones has left his said widow with two small children & no support" 20 July 1786-p. 17

"It is ordered to be further Certified to the Auditors of Public Accounts that Leannah Overstreet is the widow of John Overstreet who was an Inhabitant of Lancaster County, and who died as a Seaman in the Revenge Gally belonging to the Navy of this State about Thirty years of Age, has Five Children between the Age of Ten and Nineteen years, and is in Indigent Circumstances.

It is ordered to be further Certified to the Auditors of Public Accounts that Hannah Thatcher is the Widow of William Thatcher who was an Inhabitant of Lancaster County, and who died as a Seaman in the the Revenge Gally belonging to the Navy of this State, about Twenty four years of Age, has two children, one fourteen and the other Eleven years of age, and is in Indigent Circumstances.

It is ordered to be further Certified to the Auditors of Public Accounts that Isabella Dountain was the widow of Jesse Jent who was an Inhabitant of Lancaster County, and died as a Midshipman in the Revenge Gally belonging to the Navy of this State about Twenty Seven years of Age and Remained his widow till the 5th of June 1780 when she intermarried with William Dountain, has Five Children by the said Kent between the age of 11 and 18 years, and is in Indigent Circumstances.

It is ordered to be further Certified to the Auditors of Public Accounts that Rachel Crowder was the widow of Martin Hill, who was an Inhabitant of Lancaster County and died as a Seaman in the Ship Dragon belonging to the Navy of this State about Thirty two years of Age, and Remained his widow till the 8th of June 1780 when she intermarried with Joshua Crowder, has Two Children by the said Hill between the Age of 10 and 13 years, and is in Indigent Circumstances". 19 Oct. 1786 - p. 32

"A Certificate from the Governour to Leannah Overstreet, a pensioner, was presented in Court by the said Leannah who made oath thereto according to Law and was ordered to be recorded, and it was ordered that the Sheriff pay the same according to Law" 17 Sept. 1787 - p. 96

Order Book 1789 to 1792 (19)

"George Pitman, Jun. a Pensioner of this State exhibited to the Court a Certificate from his Excellency the Governour purporting that the said Pitman is entitled to the annual Pension of ℒ 12, and upon the said Pitman making oath that he is the person for whose benefit the said Certificate was granted, it was ordered to be recorded.

Ordered that the Sheriff pay to George Pitman, Jr. his Pension of ℒ 12 per annum for the years 1786 and 1788 It appearing tothe Court that the Pensions for these years have never been paid." 15 Feb. 1790 - p. 103

Order Book 1792 to 1799 (20)

"Ordered to be Certified to the Governor and Council that

Hannah Thatcher, widow of William Thatcher, who was a seaman in the State Navy and died in the service of this Commonwealth, is still living and is in indigent circumstances and is not of bodily ability to support herself by her own industry, and that the said William Thatcher died leaving two children from 2 to 5 years of age at the time of his death, and that by either omission or neglect the said Hannah Thatcher has been discontinued off the pension List for the year 1791" 17 Apr. 1792 - p. 12

"Ordered that it be certified to his excellency the Governor and Council that it appears from the records of this Court that there is a mistake in the Auditor's Warrant directing the payment of George Pitman's Pension for the year 1788, and that an order was duly granted by this Court for the payment of the said pension for the years 1788 & 1786 in February 1790" 18 June 1792 - p. 38

"On the motion of John Rogers this Court do Certify that the said John Rogers is the proper heir at Law of Richard Rogers, deceased, who was enlisted as a private Soldier in Captain Burgess Ball's company which was the first in the fifth Virginia Regiment and who was enlisted on the 20th day of March, 1776 as by Lieutenant Henry Towles's Certificate" 15 July 1793 - p. 109

"Ordered that it be Certified to his Excellency the Governor and Council that Jane Burne, Widow of Joseph Burne decd, (who was a Seaman in the State Navy and died in the Service of this Commonwealth) is still Living and that she is in Indigent Circumstances, and is not of Bodily ability to Support herself by her own Industry, and that the said Joseph Burne died Leaving two Children, one about three Years old and the other an Infant in the Arms at the Time of the Death of the said Joseph Burne" 16 June 1794 - p. 179

"Elizabeth Lovell, a pensioner in this County this day produced in Court a certificate from under the hand of his Excellency James Wood esquire, Whereupon it is ordered that the Sheriff do pay unto the said Elizabeth the sum of thirty pounds her pension for the year 1797" 21 May 1798 - p. 424

Orders 1808 to 1811 (23-A)
(Not paged)

"On the motion of George Broun, it is ordered that it be certified to all whom it may concern that Epaphroditus Lawson & John C. Lawson are the heirs at Law of Epaphroditus Lawson dec., late of this County" 23 Mar. 1809

"Ordered that it be certified to his excellency the Govr

& Co: of state that Sarah Ann Dye widow of John Dye decd. who by an act of the last Assembly of this State was placed on the list of pensioners, is still living in this County" 20 Nov. 1809.

"Ordered that it be certified to his excellency the Governor & Council of State, that Hannah Thatcher & Sarah Ann Dye, widow and Relict of William Thatcher, dec., a pensioner residing in this County is still living and that indigency of circumstances renders it necessary for her to be cont^d on the list of pensioners at her present allowance of £ 8 per annum" 20 Nov. 1809.

Order Book 1818-1823 (25)

"A declaration and Schedule declared and Sworn to by Joseph Locke a soldier in the Revolutionary War was made in open court and ordered to be certified to the secretary of the War Department" 18 June 1821 - p. 223

"Ordered to be certified that Richard Nicken who served in the Navy during the Revolutionary War and to whom a pension hath been allowed by the State, is living and is the same Richard Nicken on whose motion this order is made" 20 Aug. 1821 - p. 236

"Ordered to be certified to all whom it may concern that it is proved to the satisfaction of the Court by the Oaths of Ran^d Brown and Cyrus Robinson, that Sally Lewis who was Sally Cockarell, Betsy Cockarell & Nancy Cockarell are sisters and only heirs of law of Thos Cockarell dec." 19 Aug. 1822 - p. 321

Order Book from Jan. 1828 to Apr. 1834 (A-27)

"Ralph Edmonds, Addison H. Locke & Wm. C. Callahan this day in open Court made oath that Daniel Kent died intestate leaving one child Judith Currell. Jane W. Edmonds died intestate leaving the following children, Frances A. B. & Jane W. K. Edmonds. John C. Kent, son of Daniel Kent died intestate leaving one son Daniel Kent" 18 Mar. 1833 - p. 356

"It is ordered that the order made the 18 of March last relative to the heirs of Daniel Kent, dec. be amended in this "that Daniel Kent an Ensign in the Virginia line in the Revolutionary War died intestate and that no original Will of s^d Kent or any copy of any such will was ever proved or off^d for probate in this Court, and that Judith Currell, daughter of the said Daniel Kent, Frances A. B. & Jane W. K. Edmonds, children of Jane W. Edmonds, who was a daughter of Daniel Kent, & Daniel Kent son of John Kent who was a son of Daniel Kent, are the only heirs at law of the said Daniel Kent" 15 July 1833 - p. 382

"Ordered that it is certified that it is proved by satisfactory evidence adduced in Court that James Conoly, Nancy Clarke, the wife of William T. Clarke & Albert Conoly are the children and only heirs at law in fee to William Conoly late a private in the Regiment of the Virginia line" 15 July 1833 - p. 383

"It being proved to the satisfaction of the Court now sitting and the Court doth accordingly certify that Jesse George, late of this County who is reputed to have been an officer in the Virginia State Navy in the war of the Revolution, died in or about the year 1800 intestate, and that the following persons, to-wit: Sally Francis, wife of William Francis, Fanny Ford, Monroe George, Sally Frost, Elizabeth M. George, Judith D. George, Mary E. George and Alice Drummond are the only heirs at law of the said Jesse George, dec." 18 Feb. 1834 - p. 413

"It is ordered to be certified that Capt. Thomas Pollard, an officer in the Revolutionary war died intestate, and that no will or Copy of a Will has been offered for probate in this Court, and that Elizabeth T. Shanglan, Sally Kirk, Addison Hall, Felicia T. Dunaway, Ralph Edmonds, Fanny B. Edmonds, Thomas P. Hill, John Hill, Humphrey Hill, James Hill, Delia Hill, Lucy Hill, Mary Hill, Fanny Hill, Clarissa Frost, Sally Doggett & Leroy M. Pitman are the only heirs at law of the said Thomas Pollard, dec." 18 Feb. 1834 - p. 414

"Satisfactory evidence was this day adduced in Court to prove that Judith Canell, the wife of James Canell, Judith George, the wife of Jesse George, and Nancy George, the wife of Munroe George are the only heirs at law of Thomas Cox of the Revolutionary War, and that he, the said Cox, died intestate" 21 Apr. 1834 - p. 424

"Satisfactory evidence was this day adduced in open Court to prove that Elizabeth Mitchell, the wife of Thaddeus Mitchell, is the only heir at law of George Campbell, a soldier of the Revolutionary War, and that the said Campbell died intestate" 21 Apr. 1834 - p. 424

Satisfactory evidence was this day adduced in Court to prove that Elizabeth A. Allen & Sally Foster are the only heirs at law of John Allen, Sr., a soldier of the Revolutionary War who died intestate" 21 Apr. 1834 - p. 425

"Satisfactory evidence was this day adduced in Court to prove that Elizabeth A. Allen & Sally Foster are the only heirs at law of John Allen, Jr. a soldier of the Revolutionary War, who died intestate" 21 Apr. 1834 - p. 425

"Satisfactory evidence was this day adduced in Court to prove that Nicholas P. Buchan is the only devisee under the will of Spencer Hinton, dec., a soldier in the Revolutionary war." 21 Apr. 1834 - p. 426

"Satisfactory evidence was this day adduced in Court proving that Lucy T. Davenport & Nelly George, daughter of Thomas D. George only surviving Heirs of William George, dec., the said William left a son named Isaac who has not been heard from for seven to ten years and is believed to be dead, and the said William George left a will" 21 Apr. 1834 - p. 426

Orders 1834 to --------(B-28)
DD

"It being proved to the satisfaction of the Court it is accordingly ordered to be certified that William Martin who is reported to have been a revolutionary soldier, died about 1792 intestate in Lancaster County some years since, and that he left only two children, viz: Alice and Nancy Martin; Alice intermarried with a Mr. Brent & is now a widow; Nancy intermarried with Samuel M. Shearman and both died some years since intestate leaving only two children, viz: Hannah M. Shearman and Thomas W. M. Shearman; the said Hannah is now the wife of James L. Bell" 19 May 1834 - p. 2

Satisfactory evidence was adduced in Court to prove that Alfrod J. Rains, Eliza Rains, Susan Rains, Thomas S. Rains, William O. Rains, Richard Rains, Robert L. Rains & Nancy Luttrell, the wife of Richard Luttrell, Mary Ashburn, the wife of Edward Ashburn and Warner J. Rains are the only heirs at law of John Jones, a soldier of the Revolutionary War" 19 May 1834 - p. 3

Satisfactory evidence was this day adduced in Court proving that Betsey W. Lansdell, wife of John Lansdell, who was Betsey W. Spriggs, Polly Spriggs, Nathan Spriggs and Maria E. J. Corbin are the only Heirs at law of Nathan Spriggs a soldier of the Revolutionary war." 19 May 1834 - p. 3

"Satisfactory evidence was this day adduced in Court to prove that Jesse Davis & Alice Jessee, the wife of John Jessee, formerly Alice Davis, Sally Davis & Alice Davis heirs of Bartley Davis and

Cordelia Sebria, the wife of Travis Sebria, are the only heirs at law of William Davis, a soldier of the Revolutionary war who died intestate" 19 May 1834 - p. 3

"The order made at the last Term proving the Heirs of Thomas Cox is amended in this, that the name of Ran Currell be inserted in the place of Ja^S Currell" 19 May 1834 - p. 3

"Satisfactory evidence was this day adduced in Court to prove that Elizabeth Yerby and Cyrus Wilson are the only heirs at law of John Wilson who was an officer in the Navy during the Revolutionary war, and that the said John Wilson died intestate" 19 May 1834 - p. 4

"Satisfactory evidence was this day adduced in Court to prove that John Rodgers, Nathaniel C. Rodgers, Robert Daniel & Hannah his wife, who was Hannah Rodgers, and Julia Ann Connolly and Mary Connolly, children of Nancy Connolly, who was Nancy Rodgers, are the only heirs at law of John Rodgers a soldier of the Revolutionary War." 19 May 1834 - p. 4

"Satisfactory evidence was this day adduced in Court to prove that Sarah Morrison is the only heir at law of Anthony Morrison, dec^d who was a Seaman in the Navy during the revolutionary war". 19 May 1834 - p. 4

"Satisfactory evidence was adduced in Court to prove that Lucinda Phillips, formerly Lucinda Reaves, and Elizabeth Williams, formerly Elizabeth Reaves, are the only heirs at law of James Reaves dec^d a seaman in the Navy of the Revolutionary war" 19 May 1834 - p. 4

"'Satisfactory evidence was this day adduced in Court to prove that Sally Dozier, the wife of Thomas Dozier, Mary Haynie, the wife of James Haynie, Thomsey R. Thomas, Harriot Alfred, Robert Alfred, Urbane Bush, James Bush, Naomi Bush and Elizabeth Y. Bush are the only heirs at law of Thomas Bell a Sergeant in the revolutionary war." 19 May 1834 - p. 4

"John Beane, guardian to Henry and Nancy Ashbourn, is advised to make sale or transfer any Scrip that may issue to them on account of the Revolutionary services of Henry Pullin, dec." 19 May, 1834 - p. 6

"Satisfactory evidence was this day adduced in Court to

prove that Betty Weaver is the only heir at law of John Weaver dec^d a soldier of the Revolutionary war." 19 May 1834 - p. 7

"Satisfactory evidence was adduced in Court to prove that Betsy Tapore, a lunatic in the Staunton Hospital, and John Tapore are the only heirs at law of John Tapore, dec^d a seaman in the navy during the Rev'ry war" 19 May 1834 - p. 7

"Satisfactory evidence was adduced in Court to prove that Virginia P. Mitchell (formerly Virginia P. Miller), the wife of Daniel P. Mitchell, and Thos: H. Lansdell are the only heirs of John Miller, dec^d a soldier in the revolutionary war who died leaving a will which is of record" 20 May 1834 - p. 9

"It being satisfactorily proved to the Court it is accordingly ordered to be certified that John Wilson, late of Lancaster County, who is reputed to have belonged to the Virginia Navy as a Midshipman in the war of the Revolution, died intestate in this County a short time after the close of the said war, and that William Wilson was his only son and heir at Law. It also appears that the said William Wilson who is also reputed to have served in the Virginia Navy, died intestate in this County some years since, and left only two children, Cyrus L. Wilson and Betsy Baily, who are the only Heirs at law of the said John Wilson and William Wilson" 20 May 1834 - p. 10

"Satisfactory evidence was adduced in Court to prove that Dennis Dameron is the only Heir at Law of Thomas Dameron a seaman in the Navy in the revolutionary war" 20 May 1834 - p. 10

"Satisfactory evidence was this day adduced in Court to prove that Isaac, Thomas, Nancy and Catharine Pitman, children of Thomas Pitman, are the only heirs at Law of Isaac Pitman, dec^d a soldier of the Revolutionary war in Lancaster County and that (the foregoing marked out-S.N.) the children of Nancy Mahon who moved to Gloucester County" 20 May 1834 - p. 10

"Ordered that it be certified by the Court that Sally L. Findley who is a lady of respectability and strict integrity, now aged about eighty one years, this day appeared in Court and proved that Suckey Ashbourn, the wife of Luke Ashbourn, Lorenzo Roberts and William Dameron of one part, Isaac Pitman of the second part and Betsy Doggett, the wife of Elmer Doggett of the third part, are the only heirs at Law of Capt. Cyrus L. Roberts of the Continental line during the Revolutionary war; that the said Elmer Doggett & Betsy his wife moved from this County to the State of Kentucky between thirty & forty years ago, and that she does not know whether they are now living or not" 20 May, 1834 - p. 10

"It being satisfactorily proved to the Court it is accordingly ordered to be certified that Elmore Doggett, late of Lancaster County, who was in the war of the Revolution, died intestate and without issue leaving three brothers, to-wit: William, John and George Doggett. The said William died leaving five children, to-wit: Lemuel, Betsy, Alice, Maria and Griffin. The said John Doggett left three children, to-wit: Molly, Lucy and John whose heirs are now living. the said George Doggett has but one heir now living, to-wit: Thomas Doggett." 16 June 1834 - p. 14

"It is ordered that the guardians of Ralph A. Edmonds, Frances B. Edmonds, John Hill, Humphrey Hill, James Hill, Mary Hill and Fanny Hill be authorized to make sale of any land warrants or land Scrip that they may be entitled to as heirs at law of Thomas Pollard decd., a captain in the revolutionary war." 16 June, 1834 - p. 19

"Satisfactory evidence was this day adduced in Court to prove that Elijah Weaver who was in Service during the Revolutionary war died intestate, and that Elijah Weaver, Mary Pinn, Agathy Bell, Betsy Weaver and Polly Nicken, the wife of Armistead Nickin, are the only heirs at Law of Said Elijah" 15 Sept. 1834 - p. 37

"Satisfactory evidence was adduced in Court to prove that Eppa Norris is the brother and only heir of Thomas Norris, an ensign in the Continental line of the Revolutionary War, and that Thomas died intestate" 15 Sept. 1834 - p. 38

"Satisfactory evidence was adduced in Court to prove that Mary Wood and Elizabeth Kirkham are the only children and heirs at law of Joseph Wilson, a Midshipman in the Navy during the Revolutionary War" 15 Sept. 1834 - p. 38

"Satisfactory evidence was adduced in Court to prove that Juriah Harris, William H. Kirk and Elizabeth M., his wife, Polly H. Wilkins, the wife of James W. Wilkins, Sally Phillips, the wife of Bernard T. Phillips and William Rock are the grandchildren and only heirs in fee to John Harris, late a Lieutenant in the Regiment of Infantry in the Continental line." 15 Sept. 1834 - p.38

"Satisfactory evidence was this day adduced in Court to prove that Thomas Gaskins, a soldier of the Revolutionary war, died intestate and left only two children, Huldah & Mary, Huldah died intestate and without issue, Mary married William T. Champion and died leaving only one child, William G. Champion who is the only Heir at Law of the s^d Thomas Gaskins"   17 Aug. 1835 - p. 95

"Satisfactory evidence was this day adduced in Court to prove that John Miller of the County of Lancaster, a soldier of the Revolutionary war had only four children, viz: John, Thomas, Peter & Nancy; John died previous to his father without issue and intestate; Thomas died without issue and intestate; Peter died with a will & leaving several children, all of whom are dead intestate leaving no issue except Virginia P., the wife of Daniel P. Mitchell; Nancy married Thomas Lansdell and died leaving only two children, John and Thomas H.; John died without issue and left a will."   17 Aug. 1835 - p.96

"Satisfactory evidence was this day adduced in Court to prove that Luke Ashbourn is the only heir at law of Lott Ashbourn, a seaman of the State navy during the revolutionary war, and that the said Lott died intestate."   17 Aug. 1835 - p. 96

"Ordered that Cyrus Hazzard, Guardian of John Hill, Humphrey Hill & James Hill, heirs of Capt. Thos Pollard, dec^d. be authorized to make sale of any revolutionary land Scrip That the said John, Humphrey & James Hill are entitled to on account of the said Thos Pollard's revolutionary services"   21 Sept. 1835 - p. 104

"Ordered that William T. Jesse, Guardian to Mary & Fanny Hill heirs of Thos Pollard, late a Captain in the Revolutionary War, be authorized to make sale of any revolutionary Land Scrip that the said Mary & Fanny Hill may be entitled to on account of the said Thomas Pollard's services in the war of the revolution"   21 Sept. 1835 - p. 104

"Ordered that Ralph Edmonds, Guardian of Ralph A. & Frances B. Edmonds, heirs of Thomas Pollars, late a Captain in the Revolutionary war, be authorized to make sale of any revolutionary Land scrip that the said Ralph A. & Frances B. are entitled to on account of the said Thomas Pollard's services in the revolutionary war."   21 Sept. 1835 - p. 104

"Satisfactory evidence was this day adduced in open Court to prove that William Dunton, a gunners mate in the State Navy during the Revolutionary war, died in the County of Lancaster, Virginia intestate and left three children, to-wit: William, Thomas & Catharine; William is now living, Catharine is now living, and is the wife of Wm: Hammonds, Thomas died leaving a will." 21 Dec. 1835- p. 118

"It is ordered to be certified that George Currell who was in the Navy of the State of Virginia in the Rev: War in the character of Midshipman died soon after the close of the war & prior to 1787 intestate, and that John Currell was his eldest brother living at the time of Midshipman Currell's death - That the s^d John died intestate and without issue about 1787, and according to the laws of the Commonwealth his Father, who was then living and whose name was George Currell, became entitled to the estate of his son John Currell dec^d. George Currell the Father died intestate in s^d County of Lancaster in or about the year 1788, leaving several children among whom was one son Robt: Currell, to whom he gave his real estate; the s^d Robert died in s^d County testate and left his Estate to his two children Eliz$^{a.th}$ and Julius Cesar; the s^d Julius Cesar died young, the s^d Eliz^{a}th intermarried with Thos Crowder, both of whom died in 1816 leaving one child Mary Eliz^a their only heir at law, the said Mary Eliz^t intermarried with A. Hudnall of North^l County and is the heir at law of s^d Midshipman George Currell dec$^{d.}$ 18 Jan. 1836 - p. 124

"Ordered That it be certified That satisfactory evidence was this Day produced in Court to prove That Jonathan Dye, who was a Citizen of Lancaster County, enlisted in the Revolutionary War, and never returned home & was reported to have died of a wound received in that War. And it is further proven That Sarah C. Davis, formerly Sarah C. Dye,/T^{is} only heir at Law of Jonathan Dye & Sarah Ann Dye, dec$^{d.}$ 21 Mar. 1836 - p. 130

"Satisfactory evidence was this day adduced in Court to prove that Samuel Wilson of the Navy during the Revolutionary war died intestate and without issue, and left only one brother, John Wilson and the said John Wilson died intestate leaving several children all of whom died intestate and without issue except Cyrus Wilson and Elizabeth B. Yerby, formerly Elizabeth Wilson" 20 June 1836 - p. 157

"Satisfactory evidence was adduced in Court to prove that Robert Clark, a soldier of the revolutionary war, died leaving only two children, Robert and Judith; Robert died without issue, Judith married John Thrall and is since dead leaving two children, Ann who is the wife of John L. George and John who are the only heirs at law in fee to the said Robert Clark" 26 June, 1836 - p. 152

"It being proved to the satisfaction of The Court It is ordered to be certified that William Cornelius, who was said to be a gunner in the Navy of V^a in the Revolutionary War, died intestate in this County in or about the year _____ and left the following children, viz: James C., Bailey L., Sally B., who intermarried with West Cornelius, and Jane Cornelius who intermarried with John George and died intestate in or about the year _____ leaving only one child, viz: John George, Jr. It is therefore certified that James C., Bailey L., Sally B. Cornelius and John George, Senr and Joan George, J^r are The only Heirs at Law of said William Cornelius" 19 Sept. 1836 - p. 161

"It being represented to the Court that John George, Jr., (to whom James Harding was this day app^d Gd^n.) is entitled to some Military Land Scrip from the United States on account of the services of the late William Cornelius, and it appearing to the Court that it would be to the interest of the said infant that the Scrip should be sold, The Guardian above named is therefore authorized and advised by the Court to receive, sell and assign the said Scrip" 19 Sept. 1836 p. 161

"On the motion of Luke Ashbourn, who was a seaman in the Revolutionary war and who has received a pension, It is ordered to be certified that he is still living and is the same Luke Ashbourn on whose motion this order is made." 17 Oct. 1836 - p. 164

"It is proven to the satisfaction of the Court and ordered to be further certified that William Cornelius dec^d who was said to have been a gunner in the navy during the Revolutionary War died in said County of Lancaster intestate in or about the year 1813 or 1814" 19 Dec. 1836 - p. 175

"It appearing from satisfactory evidence this day produced before the County Court of Lancaster County, State of Virginia, now in session, that Sarah C. Davis, wife of Richard Davis, is sole heir at Law of Jonathan Dye and Sarah Ann Dye, late the widow of Jonathan Dye but now deceased, which is ordered to be certified" 16 Apr. 1838 - p. 261

"It is proven to The satisfaction of The Court and ordered to be certified That William Hammonds, who intermarried with Miss Catharine Dunton of Lancaster County, who was daughter of William Dunton, dec^d in The Virginia State Navy, both of whom died intestate; said Hammonds left four children, viz: William, Sarah Ann, Patsey & Eliza who are the only heirs of The said William Hammonds; and the said Sarah Ann Hammonds intermarried with Hugh Steinway and is now living in said County of Lancaster" 21 May 1838 - p. 264

"It is ordered to be certified that satisfactory evidence was this day adduced in Court to prove that George Pitman was a pensioner of the United States at the rate of eight dollars per month, was a resident of the said County of Lancaster, in the State of Virginia, and died in the County and State afs^d in the year

1815 on the 15 day of April; that he left no widow, but left three children, to-wit: Edward C. Pitman, George Pitman and William Pitman; the said Edward C. died soon after his father, William removed to parts unknown, that exertions have been made to hear from him, but have not heard from him for ten years; the said George Pitman is still living"   21 May 1838 - p. 265

"Satisfactory evidence was This day exhibited to the Court that Luke Ashbourn was a pensioner of the United States at the rate of ninety six dollars per annum, was a resident of the said County and died therein on The 24th day of December 1837, and That he left a widow whose name is Suckey Ashbourn" 18 June, 1838 - p. 274

"Satisfactory evidence has this day been produced to the Court that the papers of George Pitman a Revolutionary soldier has been burned up, and that the original certificate of pension cannot be found for surrendry, and diligent searches and enquiry have been made for it." 16 July 1838 - p. 276

"On the mo: of Saml Downing - Ordered to be certified that satisfactory evidence was this day adduced in Court to shew that Milly Jones, the widow of Lieut: Lewis Jones of the Revolutionary war was married to said Lewis on the 4" of Octo: 1789, that the s^d Lewis died on or about _____ day of Feby 1800, and that she hath remained his widow ever since; the Court further certify that Mrs: Milly Jones is a woman of strict veracity and any statement made by her is entitled to full credit" 15 Oct. 1838 - p. 288

On the motion of Same ----- Ordered to be certified that satisfactory evidence was this day adduced in Court to shew that Betsy Chilton, widow of Andrew Chilton, was married to the said Andrew on the 26" of Decr. 1785; that the said Andrew died on or about the 13" day of Novr. 1819, and that she hath remained his widow ever since - The Court further certify that the said Andrew late husband to the said Betsy, the present applicant, received a pension from the United States of account of his Rev: services - the Court doth further certify that Betsy Chilton is a woman of Veracity and her declaration may be relied on as true"   15 Oct. 1838 - p. 288

"Ordered to be certified that upon examination of the Declaration of Mrs Lucy Hubbard, widow of Charles Hubbard, dec., who was reputed to be a private in the War of the Revolution, the said Declaration was made by the said Lucy Hubbard before Charles H. Leland, one of the justices of the peace in and for said County of Lancaster in consequence of her great age and bodily infirmity which renders her unable to attend Court. In consideration of the circumstances af^d the Court approves and sanctions the said official act of the said Leland, and is or^d to be further certified that there was no record kept of marriage previous to 1794, and that there was only one marriage recorded in said Court previous to that date, and from the best information which the Court can arrive at the parish register in which all marriages were entered previous to the year 1794 is destroyed or lost. The Court further certify that upon examination of the family register that there is no record of the marriage of the said Charles Hubbard and Lucy George; that the register of births recognize them as husband and wife prior to 1794; viz: John Hubbard was born in the year 1784, Nancy Hubbard was born 13" Nov: 1783, Jesse Hubbard was born in the year 1787 on the 25" of Dec^r, and that Lucy has remained the widow of the said Charles Hubbard ever since his death" 18 Nov. 1839 - p. 354

"Ordered that it be certified that satisfactory evidence was this day adduced in Court to prove that Elizabeth Christian, late a pensioner of the United States under the Act of Congress of July 7" 1838, died on the 20th January, 1840" 18 May 1840 - p. 389

"Satisfactory proof being exhibited to this Court that Elizabeth Christian, widow of Rawleigh Christian was a pensioner of the United States at the time of his death on the 28" day of January, 1840 at the rate of eighty dollars per annum and that Ann R. Armstrong, who was Ann R. Christian before her marriage, is her child now of lawful age and resides in this County" 15 June 1840 - p. 393

"Ordered that it be certified that satisfactory evidence was this day adduced in Court to prove that Lucy Hubbard (who was the widow of Charles Hubbard, decd:) was a pensioner of the United States at the rate of seventy six dollars per annum, was a resident of Lancaster County and died therein on the 31st day of August 1840" 21 Sept. 1840 - p. 412

"Ordered that it be certified that satisfactory evidence was this day exhibited to the Court that Lucy Hubbard (who was the widow of Charles Hubbard decd:) was a pensioner of the United States at the rate of seventy six Dollars per annum, was a resident of said County and died therein on the 31st day of August, 1840, and that she left but one child living at her death, to-wit: Jess Hubbard who is still living" 19 Oct. 1840 - p. 416

Order Book 1841-1848 - (3)

"It is ordered to be certified that it is proved to the satisfaction of the Court that James Currell, who was a midshipman in the Virginia State Navy died intestate in Lancaster County about the year ____ Leaving one son, Isaac Currell, his only heir at Law, the said Isaac died intestate in Lancaster County about the year 1810 leaving sons & daughters to-wit: James, Isaac, Alice, Polly & Betsy"   17 Nov. 1845 - p. 305

"It is ordered to be certified that it is proved to the satisfaction of the Court that Daniel Kent, who was an Ensign in the Virginia line, died intestate in Lancaster County about the year 1811, leaving a son & daughters, to-wit: Judith, John and Jane his only heirs at law; the said heirs died intestate in Lancaster County leaving heirs sons & daughters, Anne B. Currell, William Currell, John L. Currell, Sarah L. Currell, Maria M. Currell and Jane Edmonds Haseltine Kent"   17 Nov. 1845 - p. 305

Ordered that it be certified that Susan Ashbourn, who is now present in Court, is still the widow of Luke Ashbourn, who was a pensioner of the United States, and that she has not married since the death of the said Luke Ashbourn, and upon her oath made the following declaration, to-wit: State of Virginia, Lancaster County, to-wit: On this 19th day of January, 1846, personally appeared before the County Court of Lancaster, Susan Ashbourn, aged about seventy years who being first duly Sworn according to law doth on her oath make the following declaration in order to obtain the benefits of the provisions made by the Act of Congress passed 7th of July 1838 granting pensions to widows of persons who served during the revolutionary war, that she is the widow of Luke Ashbourn who was a soldier in the Revolutionary War and a pensioner of the United States; she also declares that she was married to the said Luke Ashbourn after the termination of his last service in the said War and previous to the 1st of January 1794, but the exact date of her marriage she cannot ascertain in consequence of the destruction of the family record by fire in the burning of a house in which she and the said Luke Ashbourn, her husband, lived during the time of their coverture, and because marriages were not generally recorded in the Clerk's Office of this County previous to the year 1794 as shown by the certificate of the Clerk hereto appended; that her husband, the said Luke Ashbourn, died on the 24 day of December, 1838; that she was not married to him previous to his leaving the service, but the marriage took place prior to the first of January 1794 as aforesaid, she further declares that since the death of her said husband she has not been married to any other person, and that she is still a widow"   19 Jan. 1846 - p. 315

"It is ordered to be certified that it is proven to the satisfaction of the Court that Thomas Pollard who was an officer in the War of the Revolution died intestate about the year 1796, leaving the following children: Clarissa, Betsy and Sally Pollard; That Clarissa intermarried with John Hall and died leaving the following children: Addison Hall, Fanny B. Hall and Felicia T., the said Addison Hall and Felicia T., who intermarried with Thomas S. Dunaway, are still living; the said Felicia T. is now the widow of the said Thomas S.; Fanny B. Hall intermarried with Ralph Edmonds and died leaving the following children: Ralph A.

Edmonds and Fanny B. Edmonds; the said Fanny has since intermarried first with Angus Alexander, and secondly with Samuel L. Straugham, all of whom are now dead leaving children, to-wit: Robert Alexander by her first marriage and Samuel L. Straughan, Alice Straughan, who intermarried with Cyrus Haynie, Martha W. Straughan, who intermarried with Samuel Emanuel, the said Martha is dead leaving one child, to-wit: Martha S., Elizabeth Straughan who intermarried with James Lowe; the said James has since died; Jane Straughan who intermarried with Patrick Jones, Mary Straughan who intermarried with William Glasscock, who died leaving one child, William Luther Glasscock now an infant; Sally Pollard intermarried with John Kirk, both of whom are still living." 16 Feb. 1846 - p. 320

"It is proven to the satisfaction of the Court that Michael James, who was an officer in the Revolutionary war, died intestate about the year ___ ___ leaving no children but a brother, John James who died intestate leaving sons & daughters, to-wit: Thomas James, Margaret James, Mary K. James, Eliza James and William M. James. Thomas James died intestate leaving son Hiram P. James; Margaret James, who intermarried with Thomas Mason and died leaving daughter Nancy who intermarried with Custis Wessels; Mary M. James who intermarried with Joseph Barnett and Betsy James who intermarried with John Longworth, and William M. James." 16 Feb. 1846 - p. 321

"It is proven to the satisfaction of the Court that William Cornelius, who was an officer in the war of the Revolution, died intestate about the year 1812 leaving son and daughter James C. Cornelius and Sarah Cornelius who intermarried with West Cornelius, signum to the power of attorney." 16 Feb. 1846 - p. 321

"It is proven to the satisfaction of the Court that William George who was engaged in the war of the Revolution, died about the year 1800 leaving children Jesse George and Michael George." 16 Feb. 1846 - p. 321

"It is ordered to be certified that it appears to the satisfaction of the Court that Milly Jones, widow of Lewis Jones, dec., who was a Lieutenant in the war of the Revolution, was a pensioner of the United States at the rate of three hundred and sixty dollars per annum; that the said Milly Jones departed this life on the 31 day of January, 1845, and that she made and published her last will and testament by which she appointed Ralph H. Chilton and Rawleigh W. Chilton her executors; that the said **Ralph H.** Chilton took out letters of administration on the said Milly Jones estate in due form" 18 May 1846 - p. 334

Common Law Orders No. 1 - (A-28)

William Doggett, Thomas C. Dolin and Catherine, his
wife, William Berry, Martin Wilson and Judith, his wife,
John Berry, Joseph Berry, an infant, by John Berry, Sr.,
his guardian and next friend, Martin Doggett, William
Doggett, Jr., Rhoda Ann Doggett, Catharine Robinson and
Matthew Moore and Emily, his wife---------------------Plaintiffs

Against

Stafford M. Parker, Register of the Land Office of Virginia,
William Chitwood & William Helin----------------------Defendants

Removed from the Circuit Superior Court of Chancery for the
City of Richmond and County of Henrico, directing that an issue be
made up and tried at the bar of this Court.

This day came as well the plaintiffs by Richard A. Claybrook,
their attorney, as the defendants by Samuel Gresham, their attorney,
&c. Jury impaneled to determine 1st whether one or two persons of
the name of George Doggett served in the Revolutionary War;
Secondly - If there were two persons of that name who served
in the Revolutionary War whether the plaintiffs and the defendant
William Chitwood, respectively, are the heirs of the said George
Doggett, respectively, and
Thirdly - If there was but one person of the name of George
Doggett who served in the Revolutionary War whether the plaintiffs
or the Defendant, William Chitwood, are the true heirs of the George
Doggett who did so serve.

Verdict: We of the Jury find upon the first of the questions
propounded ----- that there were two George Doggetts of the County
of Lancaster employed in the Naval State Service in the Revolutionary
War.

We of the Jury find upon the second question referred to us
in the issue aforesaid, that William Chitwood is the heir of one of
the said George Doggetts, viz: the George Doggett who shipped as a
carpenter on board of the Tartar, and there being no evidence before
us in this case but what is contained in the record certified to
this Court from the Circuit Court of Chancery for the City of Richmond, and County of Henrico, We of the Jury find if the evidence in
the said record be sufficient in the judgment of the Court to est-
ablish the genealogical representation of the descendants of the
other George Doggett according to the certificates of Northumberland
and Fauquier, and to prove that the plaintiffs are the heirs of that
George Doggett, then we find that the plaintiffs are the heirs of
that George Doggett,

And as to the third question, the same is embraced in the find-
ing aforesaid"
Ordered to be certified to the Circuit Court of Chancery for

the city of Richmond and County of Henrico aforesaid. April Court, 1848 - p. 433

Order Book 1848 to 1854 (A-30)

"It is ordered to be certified that George Brent, who was reputed and believed to have been an officer in the State Cavalry during the Revolutionary War, died in this County on the 8th day of January, 1824, leaving four children, namely Fanny who is still single and alive in the aforesaid County, George P. Brent of the County of Orange, Catharine P. who married James Pollard, who together with her husband is dead leaving four children, namely William, Nancy M. who intermarried with Thomas Pinckard of Northumberland County, Catharine who has intermarried with Chatham Flowers, Sarah Ann who intermarried with Archibald Stott and died leaving the said Archibald Stott and two children, and William who is still alive, and Newton Brent who has since died leaving no issue. That the said Fanny Brent, George P. Brent, Nancy M. Pinckard, Catharine Flowers, William Pollard and Archibald Stott's two children are the only surviving heirs at Law of the said George Brent." 18 June, 1849 - p. 46

"It is ordered to be certified that it has been satisfactorily proved to this Court that Spencer Hinton, who was reputed & believed to have been a Steward in the Virginia State Navy during the Revolutionary War, died in this County in the year 1811 testate leaving Nicholas Pope Buchan his sole heir at law; that the said Nicholas Pope Buchan has since intermarried and has no issue". 18 June 1849 - p. 46

"It is ordered to be certified that it has been satisfactorily proven to this Court that Nathan Spriggs, who is reputed to have been a Carpenter in the Navy during the Revolutionary War died leaving Nathan Spriggs, Polly Spriggs & Betsy W. Spriggs as his only heirs at law" 20 Aug. 1849 - p. 53

"It is ordered to be certified that it has been satisfactorily proven to this Court that James Curtis, a Lieutenant in the Navy during the War of the Revolution, died without having married and that Albert G. Curtis, William Curtis, Hannah G. Grent, who was Hannah G. Curtis, Ann Kent, who was Ann Curtis, Alice Hughlett, who was Alice Curtis, Polly Hudnall, who was Polly Curtis, are his only heirs at law" 20 Aug. 1849 - p. 53

"It is ordered to be certified that it has been proven to the satisfaction of the Court that Michael James, who is reputed to have been a Lieutenant in the Navy during the War of the

Revolution has died leaving the following children, Polly, John, Margaret, Thomas & William M. Polly married Zanoth George and died leaving John, William P., Felicia who married _____ Barnett and Lanoth George. John married and has died leaving one child, John; Margaret married Thomas Mason and died leaving Thomas & Nancy, Nancy has intermarried with Custis Wessels; Thomas is dead leaving Hiram P. & _____; William H. is also dead leaving two children, William M. & Mary, Mary has intermarried with _____ Longwith and yet survives her husband." 17 June 1850 - p. 104

"It is ordered to be certified that satisfactory evidence was adduced in Court to prove that Col. John Fleet, Sr., who is reputed to have been a Captain in the Virginia State Line, who died intestate about 1792, left six children, to-wit: John, Sarah, Nancy, Dorothy, Betsy & Lucy Fleet." 16 Sept. 1850 - p. 120

"On the motion of Thomas Hunton, it is ordered to be certified that it appears to the satisfaction of the Court that Thomas Hunton, who was a Lieutenant in the Virginia State Navy during the war of the Revolution, departed this life the 17th day of Aug. 1792" 20 Jan. 1851 - p. 142

"On the motion of Thomas H. Hunton, it is ordered to be certified that it is proven to the satisfaction of the Court that Polly B. Hunton, who intermarried with John Gibson, who is dead leaving one child, to-wit: Albert G. Gibson her only heir at law, John W. Hunton who died unmarried and without issue, Frances Hunton who intermarried with James Brent, who died leaving two children, to-wit: William Brent and Elizabeth Brent who intermarried with William Porter, both of whom are still living; Judith M. Hunton who died unmarried and without issue; Elizabeth W. Hunton who intermarried with Sydnor McCarty, who died leaving John McCarty who has also died leaving no issue; Thomas Y. Hunton who married and is now dead leaving Susan Hunton who died unmarried and without issue; Jane F., who intermarried with William H. Brown, she has died leaving four children, Susan Jane, Ann Frances, Harriet Lee and Judith Elizabeth her only heirs, and Thomas H. Hunton are the only heirs at law of Thomas Hunton who was a Lieutenant in the Virginia State Navy during the war of the Revolution." 17 Mar. 1851 - p. 148

"It is ordered to be certified that it has been made to appear to the Court by satisfactory evidence by the oath of John Chowning, that John Payne, who was a resident in the County of Lancaster and who was a Sailing Master in the Virginia State Navy in the War of the Revolution, died in the month of July in the year 1787 or 1788, and that Edward Payne is his son and heir, and it is accordingly ordered to be certified by the Clerk of this Court." 21 Apr. 1851 p. 153

"It is ordered to be certified that John Moore, who was a sailing Master in the Virginia State Navy in the Revolutionary War died in this County on or about the ____ day of _____ 18__, leaving two children only named Ann & Judith; that Ann married a man by the name of James Bowen, who together with the said Ann, his wife, is dead leaving two children only, namely William and Judith Bowen; that the said Judith is dead without issue, and that the said William Bowen is still alive. That Judith Moore married a man by the name of William Danson, and together with her husband died leaving five children, namely John, William, Lewis, Ann and Alice; that John, William, Lewis & Alice are now living, and that Ann married a man by the name of Beverly Kent who still survives her husband." 21 July 1851 - p. 171

"It is ordered to be certified that it appears to the Court by satisfactory evidence that Daniel Kent who was an Ensign in the Virginia State Line in the Revolutionary War was a resident of this County and died therein on or about the beginning of the year 1811, leaving descendants who are citizens of this County, and to whom bounty land has been granted by the State of Virginia" 21 Feb. 1853 p. 277

"It is ordered to be certified that it has this day been proven to the satisfaction of the Court that William Dunton, alias Wm. Dawnton, who was one of the heirs at law of William Dunton, alias William Dawnton, dec., who it is reported and believed was in the Navy in the War of the Revolution, died in the year 1852, leaving a will which is of record in the Clerk's Office of this County, and his widow, Louisa Dunton, and the following children his only heirs at law, to-wit: Christopher S. Dunton, Juliet Ann Treakly who was Juliet Ann Dunton, and wife of John Treakle; Agrippa Dunton, Absdella Dunton & Theophilus Dunton, who at his death was not named, his only heirs at law; that since the death of the aforesaid William Dunton Abdella Dunton and Theophilus Dunton have died in Infancy, leaving their mother, Louisa Dunton and one whole brother, Agrippa Dunton, who is an infant under the age of 21 years, and the following half brothers and sisters, to-wit: Christopher S. Dunton and Juliet Ann Treakle, who was Juliet Ann Dunton and now the wife of John Treakle on the side of their father, and William Robbins and Mary E. Higgins, who was Mary E. Robbins on the side of their mother, their only heirs at law, and that Sarah Ann Summers, wife of Hugh Summers and Patsy Hammonds and Elizabeth Hammonds, who were other heirs at law of the aforesaid William Dunton alias Dawnton, the elder, are now living." 18 July 1853 - p. 305

"It is ordered to be certified that John Moore, who was a sailing master and Lieutenant in the Virginia State Navy during the war of the Revolution, died intestate in this County on or about the 20 day of Sept. 1802, leaving two children his only heirs at law, to-wit: Ann and Judith Moore, that the said Ann Moore married James Bowen and is dead intestate, and that William Bowen of Philadelphia is the son and only heir at law of the said Ann and James Bowen; that Judith Moore married William Danson and is dead intestate, and that John M. Danson, William Danson, Lewis Danson, Alice Danson and Ann Kent, widow of Beverly Kent, are the children and only heirs at law of the said Judith and William Danson."   19 Sept. 1853 - p. 315

"It is ordered to be certified that it appears to the Court by satisfactory proof that Thomas Hunton, formerly a Lieutenant in the Virginia State Navy in the war of the Revolution, died intestate in the County of Middlesex, Virginia, 17th day of Aug. in the year 1792, leaving six children his only heirs at law, viz: Polly B., John W., Frances, Judith M., Elizabeth W. and Thomas Y. Hunton; that Polly B. Hunton married John Gibson and is dead intestate, and that Albert G. Gibson is her only heir at law; that John W. Hunton died intestate and without issue; that Frances Hunton married James Brent and is dead intestate, and that William Brent and Elizabeth Porter, wife of William Porter, are her only heirs at law; that Judith M. Hunton is dead and left a will which is recorded in the Clerk's Office of this County (Lancaster), bequeathing her property to her brothers Thomas Y. Hunton and John W. Hunton and Elizabeth W. McCarty and nephew Albert G. Gibson & to the children of her sister Frances Brent; that Elizabeth W. Hunton married Sydnor McCarty and died intestate, leaving Jo: McCarty her only heir at law, and that said John McCarty is dead intestate and without issue, and that Thomas Y. Hunton died intestate leaving Susan, Jane F. & Thomas H. Hunton his only heirs at law; that Susan Hunton is dead intestate and without issue; that Jane F. Hunton married William W. Broun and is dead intestate, and that Susan Jane, Ann Frances, Harriet Lee and Judith Elizabeth Broun (four children) are her only heirs at law; that the said William W. Broun and Thomas H. Hunton are still living."   20 Mar. 1854 - p. 342

MUSTER ROLLS AND PAY ROLLS
Lancaster County, Virginia.
War of 1812
NINETY-SECOND REGIMENT VIRGINIA MILITIA

Muster Roll of the Field and Staff officers of the Ninety-second Regiment of Virginia Militia, commanded by Lieutenant Colonel John Chowning, in the Service of the United States at different periods during the years 1813 and 1814.

Names	Rank	Months	Days	Remarks
John Chowning	Lt. Colonel		25	
Spencer George	Major		25	
John Biscoe	"		22	
William B. Mitchell	Adjutant		25	
Thomas James	"		3	
Thomas K. Ball	Surgeon		25	
Charles Carter	Surg. Mate		19	
James Gibson	" "		6	
Wm. Lee Ball	Pay Master		25	
Ellison Curril	Qr. Master		19	
Leroy P. Leland	" "		13	
Raw. Dunnaway	Q.M.Sergt.		25	
James Kesterson	" "		9	
Joseph Shearman	" "		6	
William Pollard	" "		3	
Bidkah George	Sergt. Majr.		6	
William J. Payne	" "		19	

(For rest of this company see publication of Pay Rolls)

Muster Roll of the Militia of the Ninety-second Regiment, from Lancaster County, commanded by Major John Chowning, Jr., in service from 3d April to the 9th of the same month in the year 1813

Names	Rank	Months	Days	Remarks
John Chowning, Jr.	Major		7	
Samuel M. Shearman	Captain		7	
John Hunt	"		5	
John Biscoe	"		7	
William C. Carpenter	"		7	
Thomas Armstrong	"		7	
Thomas Yerby	"		6	
John Gaines	Lieutenant		3	
Ralph Edwards	"		5	
John Hathaway	"		7	
John Rogers	"		7	
William T. Yerby	"		7	
William H. Rogers	"		7	
William Blackstone	Ensign		7	
William B. Mitchell	"		7	
Opie Beane	"		7	

Names	Rank	Time of Service Months - Days	Remarks
James Kirk	Ensign	5	
Timothy McNamara	"	5	
Thomas Mason	Sergeant	7	
Bailey George	"	7	
John Thrall	"	7	
Nicho: P. Buchan	"	7	
James Brent	"	7	
John Kirk	"	7	
Thomas Y. Hunton	"	7	
Robert Percifull	"	7	
James Kesterson	"	7	
William T. Payne	"	7	
William George	"	7	
William Pitman	"	7	
Hilkiah Ball	"	7	
Burges K. Keen	"	7	
John Edwards, Jr.	"	7	
Leonard Stamper	"	7	
William Dunnaway	"	7	
Overton Carpenter	"	7	
Armstead T. Palmer	"	7	
John Kem	"	7	
Robert Daniel	"	7	
John Taff	Corporal	7	
James Sutton	"	7	
Joseph Wirt	"	7	
William Hill	"	7	
Walter Arms	"	7	
William Chitwood	"	7	
William Hathaway	"	7	
George Pullen	Drummer	7	
Ben: Doggett	"	7	
John Stott	Fifer	7	
Rodham Kent	"	7	
Nathaniel Alford	Private	7	
Archbald Anderson	"	7	
George Ashburne	"	7	
James Ashburne	"	7	
James Adkerson	"	7	
Thomas Bush	"	7	
Theo: Bland	"	3	
Spencer Brown	"	7	
William Boatman	"	7	
Robert Biscoe	"	7	
Charles Bailey	"	7	
Thomas Biscoe	"	7	
John Boatman	"	7	
Middleton Brent	"	7	
Newby Barrack	"	7	
William Brown	"	7	
Raleigh Brown	"	7	
Thomas P. Ball	"	7	

		Time of Service	
Names	Rank	Months - Days	Remarks
Addington Brent	Private	7	
Peter Beane	"	7	
Robert Beane	"	7	
John S. Chowning	"	7	
Thomas Coats	"	7	
William H. Chowning	"	7	
John Cundiff	"	7	
Hiram Chilton	"	7	
Stephen Chilton	"	7	
Richard Cundiff	"	7	
Thomas Christopher	"	7	
Richard Coats	"	7	
Griffin Carpenter	"	7	
Hiram Carpenter	"	7	
Robert Chum	"	7	
Richard Cockrell	"	7	
Isaac Cundiff	"	7	
John Currell	"	7	
Isaac Currell	"	7	
Thomas Cottrell	"	7	
George Carter	"	7	
Dennis Doggett	"	7	
James Doggett	"	4	
Joseph Dozier	"	7	
William Drivon	"	7	
Joseph Duvvenday	"	7	
William Doggett	"	7	
Landon Dudley	"	7	
Daniel F. Davenport	"	7	
William Dawson	"	7	
James Ewell	"	7	
William Ford	"	7	
John Flowers	"	7	
William Fleming	"	7	
James Fleming	"	7	
Thomas N. Ford	"	7	
Elias Fendley	"	7	
Isaac George	"	7	
Thomas D. George	"	7	
William Garner	"	7	
John Gresham	"	7	
John Gundry	"	7	
James Gaines	"	?	
John George	"	7	
Spencer George	"	7	
Thomas Goodrick	"	7	
Nicholus George	"	7	
William George	"	7	
Eppa George	"	7	
Martin George	"	7	
John W. Hunton	"	7	

		Time of Service	
Names	Rank	Months - Days	Remarks
Archbald Henton	Private	7	
Armstead Hayden	"	7	
Thomas Hayden	"	7	
Griffin Hayden	"	7	
Lewis Hayden	"	7	
Osburn Hayden	"	7	
Lewis Hammonds	"	7	
B. Hughlett	"	7	
John Hubbard	"	7	
George Hathaway	"	7	
Richard Hutchings	"	7	
Roystin Hughlett	"	7	
Martin Hughlett	"	7	
Richard Hinton	"	7	
Jesse Hammonds	"	7	
James Hammonds	"	7	
Thomas Hugh	"	7	
Charles Ingram	"	7	
Richard Ingram	"	7	
William James	"	7	
Charles James	"	7	
John Kemp	"	7	
James Kirk	"	7	
Westley Kirk	"	7	
James Kem	"	7	
Lodovick Kent	"	7	
Charles Kelley	"	7	
William Keebig	"	7	
Joel Kirk	"	7	
Richard Keem	"	7	
John Lowry	"	7	
Henry Law	"	7	
William Lockham	"	7	
Hiram Locke	"	7	
William Lawson	"	7	
Joseph Morgan	"	7	
Thomas Martin	"	7	
Robert Miller	"	7	
Thomas Miller	"	7	
Wm. C. McTyre	"	7	
John McNamara	"	3	
John Mason	"	7	
Thomas Mason, Jr.	"	7	
William Mason	"	7	
William Martin	"	7	
Thomas Newgeant	"	7	
Rawleigh Nover	"	7	
Robert Nutt	"	7	
Moseley Nutt	"	7	
James L. Norris	"	7	
James Nutt	"	7	
Alexander Nuwel	"	7	

		Time of Service	
Names	Rank	Months - Days	Remarks
Joseph Nutt	Private	7	
William Pitman	"	7	
William Pullen	"	7	
John Y. Percifull	"	7	
Edward Percifull	"	7	
Henry Pullen	"	7	
Edward Payne	"	7	
Isaac Pitman	"	7	
George Roberts	"	7	
James Robinson	"	7	
John Rice	"	7	
Raleigh Rains	"	7	
Richard Rant (Rout?)	"	7	
Edward Richard	"	7	
Andrew Robinson	"	7	
Lemuel Robinson	"	7	
John Richardson	"	7	
Daniel Ruse	"	7	
George Smith	"	7	
William Sutton	"	7	
Samuel Stanham	"	7	
George Spermane	"	7	
Thos: Schofield	"	7	
Daniel Shelton	"	7	
John Simmonds	"	7	
John Sampson	"	7	
William B. Sydnor	"	7	
William Simmonds	"	7	
Henry Schofield	"	7	
William Spilman	"	7	
Dempsey Treckley	"	7	
William Thrall	"	7	
Richard Towell	"	7	
George Thomas	"	7	
Thomas I. Talley	"	2	
Thornley Tankersley	"	7	
James Tankersley	"	7	
John Talman	"	7	
George Talley	"	7	
Henry Tapscott	"	7	
Thomas Thrall	"	7	
Partuer Towles	"	7	
George Welsh	"	7	
James Warwick	"	7	
Griffin Welsh	"	7	
John Walker	"	7	
Thomas L. Warwick	"	7	
John Wilder	"	7	
John Yerby	"	7	

Muster Roll

of Ensign James Brent's Company of the Ninety-second Regiment of Virginia Militia, in service from 30th November to 10th December, 1814.

Names	Rank	Time of service Months - Days	Remarks
James Brent	Ensign	11	
Thomas Y. Hunton	Sergeant	11	
Elias Fendley	"	11	
William Keeling	"	11	
Thomas Schofield	"	11	
John Flowers	Corporal	11	
James Atkerson	"	11	
Thomas Miller	"	11	
Robert Miller	"	11	
Augustine Hughlett	Private	11	
Royston Hughlett	"	11	
Anderson Hall	"	11	
Roody Miller	"	11	
Eppa Lunceford	"	11	
Thomas Oliver	"	11	
Daniel Rew	"	11	
John Richson	"	11	
Thornley Tankersley	"	11	

William C. Carpenter's Company - Ninety-second Regiment

Names	Rank	Time of Service Months - Days	Remarks
William C. Mitchell	Ensign	5	
Armistead J. Palmer	Sergeant	5	
John Gresham	"	11	
John Hubbard	"	11	
John Edwards	Corporal	11	
John Rice	"	5	
Robert Chinn	"	5	
Robert Forester	"	3	
Walter Arms	Private	14	
John Alford	"	29	
Rawleigh Brown	"	18	
William Brown	"	8	
Thomas Bean, Jr.	"	5	
John Baysay	"	11	
John Boatman	"	11	
Middleton Brent	"	20	
Richard Cockrell	"	8	
Richard Edwards	"	29	
John Flowers	"	29	
William Ford	"	29	
William Garner	"	29	
Isaac George	"	29	
Thomas D. George	"	10	
Thaddeus Goodridge	"	28	

Names	Rank	Time of Service Months - Days	Remarks
John Hutchings	Private	3	
Elias Hazard	"	8	
Hugh Hutchings	"	11	
John Knights	"	8	
George Myers	"	29	
George Mason	"	14	
Edward Pinckard	"	8	
Cyrus Pitman	"	29	
William Pitman	"	14	
John Richardson	"	29	
Alfred Rains	"	10	
Nicholas Sebre	"	18	
Michael Samuel	"	1	
Charles Simmons	"	8	
George Smith	"	29	
John M. Smith	"	14	
George Thomas	"	5	
James W. Tapscott	"	8	
Champn. Talley	"	10	
Thomly B. Tankersley	"	29	
Joseph West	"	29	

(For the rest of this company, see publication of Pay Rolls)

Captain John Hathaway's Company - Ninety-second Regiment.

Names	Rank	Time of Service Months - Days	Remarks
Thomas Biscoe	Private	5	
Thomas Carter	"	24	
Robert Daniel	"	1	
Alexander Hazard	"	24	
John Hubbard	"	7	
James Hayne	"	10	
Thaddeus Mitchell	"	20	
William Sutton	"	5	
Samuel Stoneham	"	4	
Thomas Thrall	"	5	
William Watts	"	2	
George Webb	"	10	

(For rest of this company, see publication of Pay Rolls)

Muster Roll of Lieutenant John James' Company, of the Ninety-second Regiment, Virginia Militia, in the County of Lancaster, called into actual Service under regimental orders of the 7th August, 1813.

Names	Rank	Time of Service Months - Days	Remarks
John James	Lieutenant	6	
John Kirk	Sergeant	3	

                              51
                         Time of Service
Names   Rank   Months - Days   Remarks
Coleman Doggett   Sergeant   2
Charles Kelly   "   1
James Brent   "   1
Thomas Miller   Corporal   4
John Yerby   "   4
Armistead Haydon   "   4
Elias Findley   "   4
James Ashburn   Private   4
William Driver   "   4
James Doggett   "   3
Joseph Dasher   "   1
John Flowers   "   1
James Gains   "   1
John W. Hunton   "   4
Oswell Haydon   "   4
Lewis Hammond   "   4
Bedy Hughlett   "   4
Abner Haydon   "   4
Griffin Haydon   "   3
William Keeling   "   4
Eppa Lunce   "   4
Rodolph Miller   "   1
Robert Miller   "   1
Thomas B. Oliver   "   1
John Richardson   "   2
Daniel Shelton   "   4
Thomas Schofield   "   3
James R. Tankersly "   4
Thornton B. Tankersley "   1
Joseph Talman   "   1
George Wale   "   2

          Captain James Kirk's Company - Ninety-second Regiment.
                         Time of Service
Names   Rank   Months - Days   Remarks
Richard Towell   Lieutenant   17
John James   "   6
Timothy McNamara   Ensign   23
Ellis L.B.Tapscott Sergeant   11
Thomas Mason   "   17
Coleman Doggett   "   9
Charles Kelley   "   2
John Kirk   "   3
John Thrall   "   9
Thomas Mason, Jr.   "   6
Bailey George   Corporal   17
Thomas N. Ford   "   17
Hiram Locke   "   17
Benjamin George   "   17
James Doggett   "   7

                                52
                           Time of Service
Names   Rank   Months - Days   Remarks
John Yerby   Corporal   5
Armstead Haydon   "   5
James Thrall   Drummer   17
George Pullen   "   10
James Ashburn   Private   17
Abel Alford   "   20
John Alford   "   20
Robert Bean   "   17
Thomas Bottoms   "   17
Nicholas P. Buchan   "   11
Arthur Brent   "   6
Isaac Brent   "   6
George L. Corbin   "   11
Nicholas Carter   "   17
Thomas Cottrell   "   11
George Carter   "   17
Thomas Carter   "   17
Thomas Cornelius   "   11
Isaac Currell   "   17
Isaac Currell, Jr.   "   6
Gawin Corbin   "   11
George L. Corbin   "   6
Daniel Chilton   "   7
Charles Carter   "   2
Hiram Chilton   "   4
Newman Chilton   "   6
William Driver   "   5
James Doggett   "   2
Joseph Dasher   "   2
Richard Edwards   "   10
Zamoth George   "   17
John Gains   "   17
Griffin Gains   "   17
Martin George   "   11
William Gibson   "   11
Lewis Gains   "   10
John George   "   6
Osbourn Haydon   "   7
Thomas Haydon   "   6
Griffin Haydon   "   5
Abner Haydon   "   12
Addison Hall   "   22
William Hammonds   "   17
Richard Hinton   "   11
Thomas Hughes   "   11
Augustin Hughlett   "   22
George H. Hutchings   "   8
Lewis Hammonds   "   12
Royston Hughlett   "   23
John W. Hunton   "   5
Oswall Haydon   "   5

Time of Service

Names	Rank	Months - Days	Remarks
Bedy Hughlett	Private	5	
Lewis Hammon	"	5	
Armstead Haydon	"	7	
Richard Ingram	"	11	
Charles James	"	11	
William James	"	17	
James Jefferson	"	17	
Ludwell Locke	"	17	
Eppa Lawson	"	22	
Eppa Lunce	"	5	
John Mason	"	17	
William Martin	"	11	
John McNamara	"	17	
James Mott	"	6	
Alexander Noel	"	3	
Thomas L. Norris	"	10	
James Plunket	"	12	
Cyrus Pitman	"	20	
John Roberts	"	17	
John Richardson	"	2	
Henry Schofield	"	11	
Spencer C. Smith	"	17	
Moses Short	"	20	
Charles Simmonds	"	20	
Daniel Shelton	"	5	
George Spilman	"	10	
William Thrall	"	13	
Dempsey Treacle	"	11	
Thomas Towell	"	17	
John Toleman	"	17	
John Wilder	"	17	
Thomas Yerby	"	17	
John Yerby	"	7	

(For rest of the company, see publication of Pay Rolls)

Captain Samuel M. Shearman's Company - Ninety-second Regiment.

Time of Service

Names	Rank	Months - Days	Remarks
John James	Lieutenant	6	
William George	Ensign	24	
Robert Clarke	Corporal	6	
Isaac Tilman	"	6	
John M.S. Tapscott	"	5	
Isaac Pitman	"	7	
George Gundry	Drummer	13	
Ben: Doggett	"	10	
Eppa Hill	Fifer	10	
Griffin Ashburn	Private	2 - 5	
Archibald Anderson	"	4	
Arthur Brent	"	5	

Names	Rank	Time of Service Months - Days		Remarks
Spencer Brown	Private		24	
Theodore Bland	"		10	
Theodorick Bland	"	1	1	
William Boatman	"		24	
Middleton Brent	"		24	
Robert Biscoe	"		19	
James G. Cottrell	"	2	29	
Isaac Currell, Jr.	"		5	
Gawin Corbin	"		17	
Armistead Curril	"	1	10	
Robert Clarke	"		19	
Edward Currell	"	2	8	
Jacob Currell	"		5	
James Currell	"	2	2	
Wm. H. Chowning	"		24	
John Carrell	"		10	Sub. for Henry Schofield.
John Carter	"		10	
William Danson	"		11	
Isaac Danson	"		12	
William George	"		24	
Eppa George	"		13	
William Gibson	"		10	Sub. for Wm. Spilman.
Calvin George	"		24	
Thomas D. George	"		24	
James Gains	"		24	
Jesse George	"		10	Sub. for William H. George.
James Hammond	"		7	
William Hughlett	"		6	
William Hinton	"		7	
Addison Hall	"		10	
Martin Hughlett	"		29	
Rawleigh Hazzard	"		24	
Augustin Hughlett	"		11	
Raustin Hughlett	"		4	
Charles Ingram	"		12	
John Kemp	"		12	
Richard Kemm	"		24	
James Mott	"		11	
Joseph Marryman	"		24	
Thomas Mason, Jr.	"		6	
John Mason	"		24	
Thos: B. Oliver	"		24	
William Pullen	"		24	
John Schofield	"		24	
William Spillman	"		9	
Portues Towles	"		23	
Thomas Towill	"		19	
Charles Yerby	"		10	

(For rest of this company, see publication of Pay Rolls.)

Pay Roll

of the Field and Staff Officers of the Ninety-second Regiment of Virginia Militia of Lancaster County, in the Service of the United States, from the 7th to 11th August, and from 4th to 9th December, 1813, from 21st to 23rd July, from 4th to 15th September, from 4th to 11th October, and from 30th November to 10th December, 1814.

Names	Rank	Time of Service Months - Days
John Chowning	Lieut. Col.	2 - 16
Spencer George	Major	2 - 5
John Biscoe	"	2 - 13
Wm. Lee Ball	Paymaster	1 - 29
Wm. B. Mitchell	Adjutant	2 - 3
James K. Ball	Surgeon	2 - 5
Ellison Currie	Qr. Master	1 - 16
Rawleigh Dunnaway	Q. M. Serg^t.	2 - 9
Wm. J. Payne	Serg. Major	1 - 27

Pay Roll

of Captain James Kirk's Company, of the Ninety-second Regiment Virginia Militia, Lancaster County, commanded by Col. John Chowning, for the years 1813 and 1814.

Names	Rank	Time of Service Months - Days	Remarks
James Kirk	Captain	2 - 10	
James Brent	Ensign	2 - 23	
Thomas Y. Hunton	Sergeant	1 - 22	
Elias Findlay	"	2 - 1	
John Hill	"	1 - 15	
Ralph Edmunds	"	1 - 12	
George Wale	"	1 - 1	
William Keeling	"	1 - 15	
John Richinson	"	1 - 10	Or Richardson
James Atkerson	Corporal	1 - 16	Or Atkinson
John Flowers	"	2 - 27	
Thomas Scofield	"	2 - 4	
James Gains	Fifer	2 - 2	
Martin Hughlett	Private	1 - 6	
Eppa Lunceford	"	1 - 13	
Thomas Miller	"	1 - 20	
Rhodam Miller	"	2 - 3	
Robert Miller	"	1 - 1	
Thomas B. Oliver	"	1 - 5	
Thornley B. Tankersley	"	3 - 3	
Joseph Toleman	"	1 - 7	

Pay Roll

of Captain Samuel M. Shearman's Company, of the Ninety-second Regiment of Virginia Militia, in the Service of the United States, for the years 1813 and 1814.

Names	Rank	Time of Service Months - Days			Remarks
Samuel M. Shearman	Captain	4	-	3	
Richard Towell	Lieutenant	3	-	18	
Timothy McNamara	Ensign	2	-	14	
Thomas Mason, sen.	Sergeant	4	-	3	
Ellis L.B.Tapscott	"	4	-	11	
John Thrall	"	3	-	29	
Thomas Mason, Jr.	"	4	-	23	On Guard
Thomas N. Ford	Corporal	4	-	8	
Baily George	"	3	-	24	
Ben: George	"	3	-	10	
Hiram Locke	"	4	-	10	Do.
Wm. H. George	"	3	-	4	
Thomas Yerby	"	3	-	10	
James Thrall	Drummer	2	-	18	
George Ashburn	Private	4	-	7	
James Ashburn	"	3	-	24	
Robert Beane	"	3	-	26	
Newton Brent	"	2	-	13	
Thomas Bottoms	"	3	-	20	
Nicholas P. Buchan	"	3	-	23	Do.
Geo. L. Corbin	"	3	-	13	
Nicholas Carter	"	3	-	14	
John Cornelius	"	4	-	4	Do.
Thomas Cottrell	"	3	-	29	
George Carter	"	4	-	2	
Isaac Currell	"	4			
Thomas Carter	"	5	-	1	Do.
Jas. C. Cornelius	"	2	-	23	
Aaron Danson	"	3	-	12	
Zamoth George	"	2	-	28	
John Gains	"	4	-	12	
Griffin Gains	"	2	-	18	
Martin George	"	2	-	10	
Arch'd. Hinton	"	1	-	6	Do.
William Hammonds	"	3	-	4	
Richard Hinton	"	3	-	26	
Thomas Hughs	"	2	-	24	
Jesse Hammonds	"	3	-	15	
Sam'l. Hawkins	"	1	-	9	
Richard Ingraham	"	4	-	1	
Charles James	"	3	-	8	
William James	"	2	-	9	
James Jefferson	"	3	-	19	
William Jefferson	"	2	-	7	
Griffin Ingram	"	2	-	3	Do.
George Ingram	"	1	-	16	Do.
Ludwell Locke	"	4	-	22	
Hyram Locke	"	1	-	22	Do.

Names	Rank	Time of Service Months - Days	Remarks
John Mason	Private	4 - 15	On Guard
John McNemara	"	1 - 26	
William Mason	"	4 - 21	Do.
William Martin	"	3 - 6	
John Roberts	"	2 - 28	
Joseph Shearman	"	1 -	Do.
Moses Short	"	1 - 14	Or Morris
Henry Schofield	"	3 - 17	
Spencer C. Smith	"	3 - 7	
John Scofield	"	1 - 23	
Charles Simmonds	"	24	See Capt. Thomas Yerby's Pay Roll
William Thrall	"	4 - -	On Guard
Rich'd. Treackle	"	3 - 27	
Dempsey Treackle	"	4 - -	
Samuel Treackle	"	3 - 29	
John Wilder	"	2 - 5	Do.

Pay Roll

of Captain Hugh Brent's Company, of the Ninety-second Regiment of Virginia Militia, in the Service of the United States, from 6th to 11th August, and from 3d to 9th December, 1813, from 10th to 12th and from 18th to 20th April, from 22nd April to 10th September, and from 16th September to 15th November, in the year 1814.

Names	Rank	Time of Service Months - Days	Remarks
Hugh Brent	Captain	- - -	Brent died, Wm. P. Jones was promoted to captaincy of the company
W'mson P. Jones	Captain	2 - 18	
Joseph B. Downman	Lieutenant	2 - 22	
Cyrus Ball	"	2 - 9	
George W. Downman	Cornet	2 - 22	
John Gibson	Q. M. Serg't	2 - 10	
Lawson Hathaway	Sergeant	4 - 1	
William Payne	"	2 - 23	
Bartley James	"	1 - 14	
Thomas Biscoe	"	5 - 5	
William Lawson	Corporal	2 - 12	
William Gibson	"	3 - 7	
James Brent	"	2 -	
Jesse Hubbard	"	2 - 7	
Peter Beane	Private	5 - 19	
Humphrey F. Carter	"	5 - 7	
Rawleigh Carter	"	3 - 29	
Robert Clark	"	1 - 15	
James Currell	"	1 - 21	
Lancelot B. Corbin	"	3 - 15	
Thomas Christopher	"	1 - 9	
Willis Dameron	"	2 - 29	

Names	Rank	Time of Service Months - Days	Remarks
John Edmonds	Private	5 - 10	
George England	"	1 - 29	
James Ewell	"	1 - 21	
William Eustace	"	3 - 1	
Robert Gilmour	"	2 - 13	
John Hunt	"	1 - 21	
John W. Hunton	"	4 - 6	
Richard T. Hinton	"	6 - 26	
David H. James	"	1 - 23	
John Kirk	"	3 - 26	
Arthur Lee	"	3 - 7	
Moses Lunsford	"	3 - 11	
Richard Mitchell	"	2 - 13	
Thaddeus Mitchell	"	2 - 13	
Collin Nutt	"	1 - 17	
Robert Nutt	"	2 - 27	
John Newby	"	5 - 12	
Matthew H. Oliver	"	3 - 20	
William Oldham	"	4 - 23	
Edward C. Pitman	"	3 - 1	
Richard Payne	"	2 - 7	
Robert M. Robertson	"	1 - 2	
Cornelius Sullivan	"	3 -	
Joseph Shearman	"	1 - 24	
Porteus Towles	"	1 - 10	
William L. Watts	"	3 - 25	
George Wall	"	3 - 28	
George Webb	"	2 - 1	
Griffin Webb	"	2 - 2	
Charles Yerby	"	2 - 3	

Pay Roll

of Captain William C. Carpenter's Company, of the Ninety-second Regiment of Virginia Militia, in the service of the United States, from 7th to 11th of August, and 4th to 6th of December, 1813, 23rd of April to 31st of May, 21st to 30th of June, 21st to 23rd of July, 31st of July to 15th of September, and 30th of November to 10th of December, 1814.

Names	Rank	Time of Service Months - Days	Remarks
William C. Carpenter	Captain	2 - 29	
John Rogers	Lieutenant	2 - 24	
William Callahan	Ensign	2 - 29	
Overton Carpenter	Sergeant	3 - 29	
Griffin Carpenter	"	3 - 9	
David F. Davenport	"	3 - 9	
John Kemm	"	2 - 28	
Thomas Bush	Corporal	2 - 15	

59

Names	Rank	Time of Service Months - Days		Remarks
James Kemm	Corporal	4	9	
Edward Payne	"	2	25	
Warner L. Tapscott	"	2	2	
Richard Hutchings	"	1	13	
John Hutchings	"	3	2	
Cyrus Wilson	"	3	24	
Thomas Nugent	"	3	6	
Thomas S. Warwick	Drummer	3	28	
Rodham Kent	Fifer	2	20	
Giles Eubank	"	3	9	
Wesley Kirk	"	1	8	
Burges Brown	Private	2	29	
Thomas Barns	"	1	17	
Bartley Brown	"	3	9	
Hierom Carpenter	"	3	29	
William Chitwood	"	2	2	
John Daniel	"	1	5	
Robert Daniel	"	2	24	
Daniel D. Davenport	"	3	4	
Landon Dudley	"	2	8	
James Gains	"		29	In United States Service.
Nicholas George	"	2	26	
Alexander Hazard	"	2	28	
Richard Hutchings, Jr.	"	1	18	
Cyrus Robertson	"	3	9	
Williamson B. Sydnor	"	2	7	
John Thomas	"	1	19	
David H. Tapscott	"	2	10	
Williamson Weblin	"	2	11	

Pay Roll

of Capt. John Hathaway's Company, of the Ninety-second Regiment of Virginia Militia, of Lancaster County, in the Service of the United States, from 4th December 1813 to 3d January, 1814, from 22nd April to 21 May, 1st to 11th June, 1st to 11th July, 21st to 23rd July, 7th to 11th August, 28th August to 15th October, and 30th November to 10th December in the year 1814.

Names	Rank	Time of Service Months-Days		Remarks
John Hathaway	Captain	2	15	
William Blakemore	Lieutenant	3	2	
William George	Ensign	3	2	
James Kesterson	Sergeant	3	15	
William J. Payne	"	1	29	
William Pitman	"	1	20	
John S. Chowning	"	2	24	
Charles Bailey	"	3	12	
Joseph West	Corporal	3		
Spencer Brown	"	2	27	
Richard Kemm	"	3	1	

Names	Rank	Time of Service Months - Days		Remarks
Robert Biscoe	Private	2	26	
Walter Armes	"	3	12	
William H. Chowning	"	4	16	
George Pullin	Drummer	3	13	
John Alfred	Private	1		
Abel Alfred	"	1		
Allington Brent	"	1	21	
John Bailey	"	1	23	
William Boatman	"	3	2	
Thomas Bush	"	1		
Burgis Brown	"	1		
Bartley Brown	"	1		
Middleton Brent	"	1		
John Boatman	"	1		
William Chitwood	"	4	9	
Hiram Carpenter	"	1		
William Chitwood	"	1		
Landon Dudley	"	1		
Daniel D. Davenport	"	1		
Giles Eubank	"	1		
Richard Edwards	"	1		
John Edwards, Jr.	"	1		
William Ford	"	3	6	
Calvin George	"	3	29	
Isaac George	"	2	20	
William Garner	"	1	19	
Thomas D. George	"	3	6	
Nicholas George	"	1		
William Hill	"	2		
Rawleigh Hazard	"	1	13	
Richard Hutchings	"	1		
John Hutchings	"	1		
James Kemm	"	1		
Joseph Merryman	"	2	5	
John Mason	"	1	13	
George Myers	"	2	24	
Cyrus Newby	"	1	4	
Thomas Newgent	"	1		
William Pullen	"	3	29	
Edward Payne	"	1		
Cyrus Pitman	"	1		
Cyrus Robertson	"	1		
George Smith	"	3	29	
John N. Smith	"	1	18	
Portues Towles	"	1	10	
John Thomas	"	1		
Griffin Webb	"	1	1	
James Warwick	"	3	21	
Cyrus Wilson	"	1		
Williamson Wiblin	"	1		

Pay Roll of Captain William T. Yerby's Company, of the Ninety-second Regiment of Virginia Militia, Lancaster County, in the Service of the United States, commanded by Lieutenant Colonel John Chowning, for the year 1814.

Names	Rank	Time of Service Months - Days	Remarks
William T. Yerby	Captain	4 - 10	
Armistead J. Palmer	Lieutenant	3 - 24	
James Robinson	Ensign	4 - 2	
William Stott	Sergeant	4 - 4	
John Edwards	"	3 - 26	
William Simmonds	"	3 - 22	
Charles J. Yerby	"	4 - 17	See Captain Thomas Yerby's
Hilkiah Ball	Corporal	3 - 4	Pay Roll
Thomas Christopher	"	4 - 4	
James Talley	"	3 - 25	
Thomas Martin	"	4 - 5	
John Gundry	Drummer	2 - 21	
Eppa Hill	Fifer	2 - 21	
Thomas Beane	Private	2 - 21	
John Boatman	"	- - 24	Not sufficient time on this roll.
Isaac Cundiffe	"	4 - 10	
Richard Cockarill	"	4 - 7	
Richard Cundiffe	"	4 - 10	
Hyram Chilton	"	3 - 29	
Griffin Chilton	"	4 - 12	
Addison Connolly	"	3 - 7	
Wm. C. Callahan	"	4 - 15	
Daniel Chilton	"	1 - 29	
Stephen Chilton	"	2 - 21	
Richard Dunnaway	"	4 - 3	
Dennis Doggett	"	3 - 13	
David Edwards	"	3 - 25	
Robert Forrester	"	2 - 17	
John Hunt	"	1 - 13	
John C. Hinton	"	3 - 18	
Wm. O. Hayden	"	3 - 13	
Thomas Hayden	"	1 - 6	
Jesse Kent	"	3 - 26	
Joel Kent	"	4 - 7	See Capt. Thomas Yerby's pay
Lodowick Kent	"	3 - 29	roll.
Charles Kelly	"	4 - 28	
Wesley Kirk	"	3 - 22	
James Mitchell	"	3 - 26	
George M. Mitchell	"	3 - 24	
John W. Mitchell	"	4 - 2	
James Nutt	"	3 - 25	
Moseley Nutt	"	3 - 27	Do. Do.
Joseph Nutt	"	3 - 14	
John Y. Percifull	"	3 - 22	
Edward Pinckard	"	4 - 11	
Albert J. Raines	"	2 - 22	

Names	Rank	Time of Service Months - Days		Remarks
John Sampson	Private	4	6	
Daniel Shelton	"	2	-	Or Chilton
Samuel Stoneham	"	4	-	
John Talley	"	3	28	
Henry Tapscott	"	3	20	
Thomas J. Tally	"	2	15	
George Talley	"	3	26	
Warner L. Tapscott	"	2	17	
Benjamin Walker	"	4	7	

Pay Roll of Captain Thomas Yerby's Company, of the Ninety-second Regiment of Virginia Militia, Lancaster County, Commanded by Lieut. Col. John Chowning, for the years 1813 and 1814.

Names	Rank	Time of Service Months - Days		Remarks
Thomas Yerby	Captain	1	5	
John Alford	Private	1	15	
Abel Alford	"	-	25	Time not sufficient on this roll, but served also in Capt. James Kirk's Company.
Middleton Brent	"	1	-	
Richard Edwards	"	-	20	Do do do
Royston Hughlett	"	-	5	Do do and Capt. Shearman&s Company.
Lodowick Kent	"	1	-	See Capt. Wm. T. Yerby's pay roll
Joel Kent	"	1	-	Do do do
Moseley Nutt	"	1	-	Do do do
James L. Norris	"	-	-	See Capt. James Kirk's pay
Cyrus Pitman	"	1	6	roll
Moses Short	"	-	10	See Captains Kirk's and Shearman's pay rolls.
Charles Simmonds	"	-	20	Do do do
George Spilman	"	-	25	See Capt. Kirk's pay roll
Charles J. Yerby	"	1	-	See Capt. Wm. T. Yerby's pay roll.

Pay Roll of Captain Thomas Armstrong's Company, of the Ninety-second Regiment of Virginia Militia, in the Service of the United States, during the years 1813 and 1814.

Names	Rank	Time of Service Months - Days		Remarks
Thomas Armstrong	Captain	2	5	
William H. Rogers	Lieutenant	4	7	
Opie Dunaway	"	4	9	
Thomas Shearman	Sergeant	3	28	Thos: Mason his sub.
Thomas Mason	"	1	-	Sub. for T. Shearman.

Names	Rank	Time of Service Months - Days			Remarks
Thomas G. Robertson	Sergeant	4	-	20	
Andrew Robertson	"	4	-	17	
Robert Percifull	"	4	-	8	
James Brent	"	3	-	26	
John Taff	Corporal	4	-	8	
William Hathaway	"	3	-	24	
William Fleming	"	4	-	14	
William Hinton	"	3	-	15	
Benjamin Doggett	Drummer	5	-	13	
William Luckham	Fifer	5	-	5	
Nathan Alford	Private	3	-	17	Thos. N. Ford his sub.
Griffin Ashburn	"	3	-		Sub. for Geo. Thomas.
Newby Berrick	"	5	-	13	
Kenner Brent	"	5	-	12	
George Brent	"	4	-	22	
Thomas Beane	"	3	-	3	
Rawleigh Brown	"	4	-	18	
John Barnett	"	3	-	17	
William Brown	"	4	-	8	
Jesse Bailey	"	2	-	24	
William Berrick	"	3	-	1	
Isaac Currell	"	-	-	10	Sub. for V. Thomas
Richard Coats	"	4	-	5	
Thomas Coats	"	4	-	17	
Robert Chinn	"	4	-	12	
Thomas Cockarell	"	3	-	18	Sub. for Cyrus Pitman
James Cornelius	"	-	-	22	Sub. for V. Thomas
Richard Dodson	"	4	-	9	
Joseph Dunnaway	"	4	-	23	
Charles Doggett	"	2	-	21	
William Driver	"	3	-	9	
Coleman Doggett	"	2	-	23	
William Danson	"	2	-	10	
Cyrus Edwards	"	5	-	3	
Thomas N. Ford	"	1	-	7	Sub. for Nathan Alford
James Flemming	"	3	-	1	
Lawson George	"	2	-	24	Sub. for Wm. Reviere
James Gaines	"	2	-	13	Do do do
William Gibson	"	1	-	10	
John George	"	2	-	5	
George Hathaway	"	3	-	11	
Griffin Haydon	"	3	-	15	
Armstead Haydon	"	3	-	1	
Abner Haydon	"	4	-		
Osmand Haydon	"	4	-	9	
William Hill	"	3	-	26	Sub. for Wm. Sims
Archibald Hinton	"	3	-	4	
Lewis Hammond	"	2	-	7	
Addison Hall	"	1	-	29	Sub for Francis Potts.
Charles Haydon	"	3	-	21	
George Ingram	"	3	-	26	

Names	Rank	Time of Service Months - Days		Remarks
Griffin Ingram	Private	2	24	
James Kirk	"	2	15	
Thomas Lunsford	"	4	4	
Eppa Lawson	"	1	17	
Wm. Mason	"	1	20	Sub. for W. Dunnaway
Thomas Mason, Jr.	"	1		Sub. for Wm. Danson
John Mason	"	1		Sub. for C. Doggett
Rawleigh Norris	"	4	12	
Richard Norris	"	4	11	
Presley Neale	"	3	7	
Robert Pitman	"	4	18	
Cyrus Pitman	"	2	22	Thos: Cockarell sub.
William Pitman	"	2	5	
Edward Percifull	"	4	11	
Francis Potts	"	-	8	Addison Hall his sub.
Joel Riviere	"	2	17	
Cyrus Riviere	"	4	8	
Richard Routt	"	3	28	
James Riviere	"	3	22	
William Riviere	"	2	15	
William Sims	"	2	11	Wm. Hill his sub.
Ahimes Sullivant	"	3	18	
Moses Short	"	1	22	
Spencer Smith	"	1	-	Sub. for Wm. Riviere
George Thomas	"	1	21	Griffin Ashburn sub.
Vinvent Thomas	"	1	23	Isaac Currell his sub.
John Toalman	"	2	17	
John Walker	"	2	24	
Samuel Wall	"	3	-	
Spencer Watts	"	3	13	

Adkerson(Atkerson-Atkinson)
James 45,49,55

Alexander,Angus 38; Fanny B. 38;
Robert 38

Alford(Alfred) Abel 52,60,62;
Harriot 29; John 49,52,60,62;
Nathan *63; Nathaniel 45;
Robert 29

Allen, Elizabeth A. 27, 28; John,
Sr. 27; John,Jr. 28

Arms(Armes) Walter 45,49,60

Armstrong, Ann R. 36; Thomas 44;
Capt. Thomas *62

Anderson, Archibald 45,53

Ashburn(Ashbourn) Edward 28;George
45,56;Griffin 53,63,64;Henry 29;
James 45,51,52,56;Lott *32;Luke
30,32,*34,35,*37;Mary 28;Nancy
29;Suckey 30,35;Susan 37

Bailey(Baily) Capt. 2;Betsy 30;
Charles 45,59;Edward 21;Jesse 63;
John *2,16,20,60;William Newby 21;

Ball,Agatha 11;Capt.Burgess 25;
Cyrus 57;Hilkiah 45,61;James 1,*4,
*18,21;James,Jr. 1,*2,*4,*6;James
K. 55;Col. James 13,14;Col.Jesse
*1;Margaret 13;Rich^d. 14;Thomas
K. 44;Thomas P. 45;Dr.William 13,
21; William Lee 44,55

Barnett,Filicia 41;John 63;Joseph
38;Mary K. 38

Barrack,Newby 45

Baysay, John 49

Bean(Beane) John 11,29;Opie 44;Peter
46,57;Robert 46,52,56;Thomas 61,
63;Thomas,Jr. 49;William 16

Beale,Elizabeth 20

Belvaird,Robert 16

Bell,Agathy 31;Charles 10,15;
James L. 28;Thomas 29

Berry,John 39;John,Sr.39;Joseph
39;William 39

Berrick,Newby 63;William 63

Berryman,John 1,*3,12,14

Biscoe,Eliz^a: 16;John *44,55;
Robert 45,54,60;Thomas 45,50,
57

Bland,Theo: 45;Theodore 54;
Theodorick 54

Blackstone,William 44

Blakemore,Edward 2,3,13;Jemima
13,19;William 59

Boatman,John 45,49,60,61;
William 13,45,54,60

Bond, Sarah 10

Bottoms,Thomas 52,56

Boulware,Thos: 16

Bowen,Ann *42,43;James *42,
43;Judith 42;William *42

Boyd,David 1;John 14

Brent,Mr.28;Addington 46;
Allington 60;Arthur 52,53;
Catharine P. 40;Elizabeth 41;
Fanny *40;Frances 41,*43;
George *20,*40;George P. *40;
Hugh 1;Capt. Hugh *57;Isaac
52;James 12,15,20,41,43,45,49,
51,55,57,63;John 22;Judith 13,
15;Kenner 63;Middleton 45,49,
54,60,62;Newton 4,14,40,56;
Richard 22;Thomas 15;William
9,41,43

Brown(Broun)Ann Frances 41,43;

Bartley 59,60;;Burges 59,60;
George 25;Harriet Lee 41,43;
James 16;Jane F.(I?) 41;John
*5,*6,*7,16;Judith Elizabeth 41,
43;Raleigh 45,49,63;Ran^d:26;
Spencer 14,45,54,59;Susan Jane
41,43;William 1,10,15,21,45,49,
63;William W. 41,*43

Buchan,Nicholas P. 28,45,52,56;
Nicholas Pope *40

Burwell,Nathaniel 17

Burn(Burne) Jane 22,25;Joseph *25

Bush,Elizabeth W. 29;Naomi 29;
Thomas 45,60;Urbane 29

Callahan,William 58;William C.26,
61;

Campbell(Cammell),George 8,14,*27

Canell,James 27;Judith 27

Carter,Capt.2;Charles 17,19,44,52;
Edward 10,16;George 15,46,52,56;
Harry 11;Humphrey F. 57;Job 8,16;
John 11,15,54;John Hill 7;Joseph
19;Nicholas 52,56;Rawleigh 57;
Thomas 1,12,14,15,18,*19,50,52,
56;Capt. Thomas *2

Carpenter,Griffin 46,58;Hiram 46,59,
60;Overton 45,58;William 10,14;
William C. 44;Capt.William C. 58;

Carrell(Currell?) John 54

Champion,Mary 32;William C. 32;
William T. 32

Chilton,Andrew *35;Betsy *35;Daniel
52,61;Griffin 61;Hiram 46,52,61;
Jesse 13;John 9,14;Newman 52;
Ralph H. 38;Rawleigh W. 38;Stephen
11,46,61;William 10

Chitwood,William *39,45,59,*60

Chinn,John 1,6,15;Robert 14,49,
63;Capt.Robert 2,8

Chowning,John *2,3,12,41;John S.
46,59;Lt.Col.John *44,*55,60;
Maj. John,Jr. *44;William 1,
12,20;William H. 46,54,60

Christopher,Thomas 46,51,61;

Christian,Ann R. 36;Elizabeth
*36;Rawleigh 36

Chum(Chinn?) Robert 46

Clark(Clarke)Judith *33;Nancy
27;Robert *33,53,54,57;
William T. 27

Clayton,John 8,15

Claybrook,Richard A. 39

Coats,Richard 46,63;Thomas 46,
63;

Cockarell(Cockarill)Betsy 26;
Nancy 26;Richard 46,49,61;;
Sally 26;Thos 26,63,64;

Conway,Edwin 1,*2,*4;Col.Edwin
8,14;;Peter 14,16;

Connolly(Conoly)Addison 61;
Albert 27;James 27;Julia Ann
29;Mary 29;Nancy 29;William
27

Corbin,Gawin 52,54;George L.
*52,56;Launcelot B. 57;Maria
E.J.28

Cornelius,Bailey L. 33,34;
James 63;James C. 33,34,38,
56;Jane 33;;John 56;Sally B.
33,34;Sarah 38;Thomas 52;
West 33,38;William 33,*34,38

Cottrell,James G. 54;Thomas 46,
52,56

Cox,Thomas *27,29

Crowder, Elizabeth 33; Joshua 23,24; Rachel 23,24; Thos: 33;

Cundiff, Isaac 46,61; John 11,46; Rich^d 14,46,61;

Currell(Curril) Alice 37; Anne B. 37; Armistead 54; Betsy 37; Edward 54; Ellison 44; Elizabeth *33; George 18,*33; Henry 8,15; Isaac *15,36, 37,46,52,56,63,64; Isaac,Jr. 52, 54; Jacob 54; James 15,29,36,37,54, 57; James,Jr.15; John *33,46; John Z. 37; Judith *26; Julius Cesar *33; Maria K. 37; Mary Eliz^a: *33; Nicholas 6,*7,9,15,17; Polly 37; Robt: *33; Sarah L. 37; William 37

Currie, Rev. David 7; Ellison 55

Curtis, Albert G. 40; Alice 40; Hannah G. 40; James 40; Polly 40; William 40

Dameron, Aaron 23; Dennis 30; Thomas 30; Willis 57; William 30;

Danson, Aaron 56; Alice 42,43; Ann 42; Isaac 54; John 42; John M. 43; Judith 42,*43; Lewis 42,43; William *42,*43, 43,63,64;

Daniel, Hannah 29; John 59; Robert 29, 45,50,59;

Davenport, Daniel D. 59,60; Daniel F. 46; David F. 58; Lucy T. 28

Davis, Alice *28; Bartley 28; James 23; Jesse 28; John 11,15; Richard 34; Sally 28; Sarah C. 33,34; William 29

Dawson, Henry 15; Mary 15; William 46

Dawnton(Dunton-Dountain) William *42

Degges(Degge) Isaac 1,*2,15,19

Denison, Jonathan 19

Dobbs, Joseph 11,15,17

Dodson, Richard 63

Doggett, Alice 31; Benjamin 45,53, 63; Betsey *30,31; Charles 63; C. 64; Coleman 11,16,*51,63; Dennis 46,61; Elmer *30; Elmore 10,20,31; George *31,*39; Griffin 31; James 46,*51,52; John *31; Lemuel 31; Lucy 31; Maria 31; Martin 39; Molly 31; Rhoda Ann 39; Sally 27; Thomas 31; William 13,15,*31,39,46; William,Jr. 39;

Dolin, Catherine 39; Thomas C. 39

Dountain(Dawnton-Dunton) Isabel 23,24; William 23,24

Downman, George W. 57; Joseph B. 57; Raw^h 8,15;

Downing, Sam'l. 35

Dozier(Dasher) Joseph 46,51,52; Sally 29; Thomas 29

Driver(Drivon) 46,51,52,63

Drummond, Alice 27

Dudley, Landon 46,59,60

Dunton(Dawnton-Dountain) Ab^{s}della *42; Agrippa *42; Catharine *32,34; Christopher S. *42; Juliet Ann *42; Louisa *42; Theophilus *42; Thomas *32; William *32,34,*42

Dunaway, Felicia T. 27,37; John 22; Joseph 63; Opie 62; Raw: 44,55; Richard 61; Thomas 14; Thomas S. *37; William 12,22, 45; W. 64;

Duvvenday, Joseph 46

Dye, John 26; Jonathan *22,*33, 34; Nancy 22; Sarah Ann 22, *26,33,34; Sarah C. 33

East,Rich^d 9

Eddings,Capt. Sam'l. 8,*9

Edmonds(Edmunds)Elias *2,7;Fanny B. 27,31,*32,*38;Frances A. B. *26;Jane 37;Jane W. *26;Jane W. K. *26;John 58;Ralph 26,32,37, 55;Ralph A. 31,*32,37;

Edwards,Cyrus 63;David 61;John 49, 61;John, Jr. 45,60;Ralph 44; Richard 49,52,60,62;William 11;

Emanuel,Martha S. 38;Martha W. 38; Samuel 38

England,George 58

Eubank,Giles 59,60

Eustace,John 13,18;William 58

Ewell,James 1,*2,16,46,58;Capt. James 7

Fauntleroy,Moore 11

Fendley(Findley)Elias 46,49,51,55; Sally L. 30

Fleet,Betsy 41;Dorathy 41;John 1,4, *18,41;Col. John 9,21;Col.John,Sr. 41;Lucy 41;Nancy 41;Sarah 41;

Flemming(Fleming)James 13,46,63; William 46,63

Flint,Thomas 9,16

Flowers,Catharine *40;Chatham 40 John 4,6,15,46,49,51,55

Ford,Fanny 27;Thomas N. 46,51,56,*63; William 46,49,60

Forrester,Robert 49,61

Foster,Sally 27,28

Frost,Clarissa 27;Sally 27

Francis,Sally 27;William 27

Gains(Gaines)Griffin 52,56;James 46,51,54,55,59,63;John 44,52, 56;Lewis 52

Galloway,Milly 3

Garner,William 46,49,60

Garland,Thos 17

Gaskins,Huldah 32;Mary 32;Thomas 31,32

George,Ann 33;Bailie *1,4,6,14,45, 51,56;Benjamin 12,51,56;Bidkah 44;Calvin 54,60;Elizabeth M. 27; Eppa 46,54;Felicia 41;Isaac 28, 46,49,60;Jane 33,34;Jesse 8,16, *27,38,54;John 33,41,46,52,63; John,Jr. *34;John M. 33;Judith 20,27;Judith D. 27;Lamoth 41; Lawson 63;Lucy 36;Martin 15,46, 52,56;Mary E. 27;Michael 38; Monroe *27;Nancy 27;Nelly 28; Nicholas 8,16,*21,46,59,60; Polly 41;Spencer 1,44,46,55; Thomas D. 28,46,49,54,60; William 16,28,38,41,45,46,53, 54,59;William H. 56;Zamoth 41, 52,56

Gibson,Capt. 4;Albert G. 41,*43; James 44;John 41,43,57;Polly B. 41,43;William *2,3,15,52,*54, 57,63

Gilmoure,Robert 9,20,58

Glasscock(Glascock)Mary 38; William 38;William Luther 38

Goodrick,Thomas 46

Goodridge,Joseph 16;Rich^d 8,14; Thaddeus 49

Gordon,James *1,*2,*4,*6,17; Col. James 10,14,17;Nathaniel 10

Gresham,John 46,49;Samuel 39

Griffin,Thomas B. *1;Col.William 6,*7,*17

Griggs,William 9,15

Gundry,George 53;John 46,61

Guthrie,George 7;Sam'l. 6,8

Hall,Addison 27,*37,52,53,63,64; Anderson 49;Clarissa 37;Fanny B. *37;Felicia T. *37

Hammonds(Hammond-Hammon)Catharine 32,34;Elizabeth 34,42;James 47,54;Jesse 47,56;Lewis 47,51,52,53,63;Patsey 34,42;Sarah Ann *34 Wm: 32,*34,52,56;

Harding,James 34

Harvey,Mungo 9,18

Harris,John 12,31;Juriah 31;

Hathaway,John 44;George 47,63; Capt. John 50,*59;Lawson *2,16,57;Thomas 1,2,16;William 45,63

Hawkins,Sam'l. 56

Haydon(Hayden)Abner 51,52,63; Armstead 47,51,52,53,63;Charles 63;Griffin 47,51,52,63;Lewis 47; Mary 12;Osburn(Osmand) 47,52; Oswell 51,52;Thomas 47,52,61; William O. 61

Haynie(Hayne)Alice 38;Cyrus 38; James 29,50;Mary 29;

Hazard(Hazzard)Alexander 50,59; Cyrus 32;Elias 50;Rawleigh 54,60

Helin,William 39

Henry,Patrick 2

Higgins,Mary E. 42

Hill,Betty 16;Delia 27;Elizabeth 11;Eppa 53,61;Fanny 27,31,*32; Humphrey 27,31,*32;James 27,31,*32;John 27,31,*32,55;Lucy 27; Mary 27,31,*32;Martin 23,24; Rachel 3;Thomas P. 27;William 45,60,63,64;

Hinton(Henton)Archbald 47,56,63; Harry 15;Henry 12;John C. 61; Richard 47,52,56;Richard T. 58; Spencer 28,40;William 19,54,63

Hubbard,Charles 35,*36;Jesse *36, 57;John 36,47,49,50;Joseph 14; Joshua 10;Lucy *35,*36;Nancy 36; Thomas 9

Hudnall,A. 33;Mary Eliz^a: 33; Polly 40

Hughes(Hugh)Thomas 47,52,56

Hughlett,Alice 40;Augustine 49,52,54;B. 47;Bedy 51,53;Martin 47,54,55;Raustin 54;Roystin 47,49,52,62;William 54;

Hunton,Elizabeth W. 41,*43; Frances 41,*43;Jane F.(I?)*43; John W. 41,*43,46,51,52,58; Judith M. 41,*43;Polly B. 41,*43;Susan 41,43;Thomas 12,14,*18,19,*41,43;Thomas H. *41,*43;Thomas Y. 41,*43,45,49,55;

Hunt, John 44,58,61

Hutchings,George H. 52;Hugh 50; John 50,59,60;Richard 47,59,60;Richard,Jr. 59

Ingram,Charles 47,54;George 56,63;Griffin 56,64;Richard 47,53,56;Thomas 20

Jacob, Robert Clark 7;Robert C. 20

James, Bartley,57;Betsy 38;Charles 47,53,56;David H. 58;Eliza 38; Elizabeth 14;Eliz[a]: Jr. 15Hiram P. 38,41;John 15,38,*41;Lt. John *50,53;Mary 41;Mary K. *38; Margaret *38,*41;Michael 38,40; Polly 41;Sarah 15;Thomas *38,*41, 44;William 47,53,56;William M. *38,*41;

Jefferson,James 53,56;Thomas 4; William 56

Jessee,Alice 28;John 28;William T. 32

Jones,Jane 38;John 28;Lewis 23; Lt.Lewis *35,38;Milly *35,*38; Nancy 23;Patrick 38;W'mson P. *57

Keeling,William 49,51,55

Keebig,William 47

Keen,Burges K. 45

Kelley,Charles 47,*51,61

Kem(Kemm-Keem)James 47,59,60; John 45,59;Richard 47,54,59

Kemp,John 47,54

Kent,Ann 42,43;Beverly 42,43; Daniel *26,*27,37,42;Haseltine 37;Isabel 3;Jane 37;Jesse *3, 23,*24,61;Joel 61,62;John 26,37; John C. 26;Judith 37;Lodovick 47, 61,62;Rodham 45,59

Kesterson,James 44,45,59

Kirkham,Elizabeth 31

Kirk,Elizabeth M. 31;James 10,47, 64;Capt.James 45,51,*55,*62; Joel 47;John 38,45,50,51,58; Sally 27,38;Westley 47,59,61; William *3,4,6,15;William H. 31

Knights, John 50

Lansdell,Betsey W. 28;John 28,32; Nancy 32;Thomas 32;Thomas H.32; Thomas R. 30

Law,Henry 47

Lawson,Epaphroditus *25;Eppa 53, 64;Henry 1,3,4,8,*18; H. 13; John C. 25;Mary 8,18;Thomas *1, 9,15;William 15,47,57

Lee,Arthur 58;Charles 15,20; Richard *20;Richard E. 1; Thomas 13

Leland,Charles H. 35;Rev.John 14; Leroy P. 44

Lewis,Sally 26

Lizenby,Ellen 11

Locke(Lock)Addison 26;Hiram 47, 51,*56;Joseph 26;Ludwell 53, *56;Stephen 14

Lockham,William 47

Longwith,John 12,15,19;Mary 41

Longworth,Betsy 38;John 38

Lovell,Elizabeth *25

Lowe,Elizabeth 38;James *38

Lowry,Gawin 10;John 47

Luckham,William 63

Lunce,Eppa 51,53

Lunceford(Lunsford)Eppa 49,55; Moses 58;Rodham 16,*19;Thomas 64

Luttrell,Nancy 28;Richard 28

McCarty,Charles 21;Elizabeth W. 41,43;John 41,43;Jo: 43;Sydnor 41,43;Thadeus 1,6,13,17,21

McNamara,John 47,53,57;Timothy 45, 51,56

McTyre,Elizabeth 9,15;John 4,15; William C. 47

McWilliams,John 16

Mahon,Nancy 30

Markham,Capt. James *23

Martin,Alice 28;Nancy 28;Thomas 47,61;William 12,18,28,47,53,57

Mason,George 50;John 47,53,54,57, 60,64;Margaret 38,41;Nancy 38, 41;Thomas 38,*41,45,51;Thomas,Sr. 56;Thomas,Jr.47,51,54,56,62,64; William 15,47,57,64

Marryman(Merryman)Joseph 54,60

Merideth,John 14;William 12

Miller,John 8,16,30,*32;Nancy *32; Peter *32;Rodham 55;Robert 47,49, 51,55;Rodolph 51;Roody 49;Thomas *32,47,49,51,55;Virginia P.30, 32

Mitchell,Daniel P. 30,32;Elizabeth 27;George M. 61;James 61;John W. 61;Richard 1,3,4,5,14,16,58; Thaddeus 27,50,58;Virginia P. 30, 32;William 15;William B. 44,55; William C. 49

Montague,William 14

Moore,Ann *42;Emily 39;John *42; Judith *42,43;Matthew 39

Morgan,Joseph 47;

Morrison,Anthony 29;Sarah 29

Mott,James 53,54

Myers,George 50,60;Matthew 10,17, *19;Thomas 10,19

Nason,Nat 5,6

Naughton,John 15

Nawel, Alexander 47

Neale,Presly 16,64

Nelson,Thomas *4,10

Newgent(Newgeant-Nugent)Thomas 47,59,60

Newby,Cyrus 60;George 23;James 9,14;John 21,23,58;Leroy 21; Ozwals 14;W^{m}son 23

Nicken,Armistead 31;Polly 31; Richard *26

Noel,Alexander 53

Nover,Rawleigh 47

Norris,Eppa 31;George 10,15; James 14;James L.47,62;John 16;Joseph 10,16;Rawleigh 64; Richard 64;Thomas *31;Thomas L. 53

Nutt,Collin 58;James 47,61;Joseph 48,61;Moseley 47,61,62;Robert 47,58

Oldham,William 58

Oliver,Matthew H. 58;Thomas 49; Thomas B. 51,54,55

Overstreet,John 22,*23;Leannah 3,22,*23,24

Palmer,Abner 11,16;Armistead J. 49,61;Armistead T. 45;Lott 2, 3,4;

Parker, Stafford H. 39

Parrett,John 14,15

Payne,Edward 41,48,59,60;John 16, 18,41;Richard 58;William 57; William J. 44,55;William T. 45,59

Percifull,Edward 48,64;Elijah 3, 15,13,21;;John Y. 48,61;Robert 45,63

Perkins,Ann 23;Elizabeth 23; James 23;Thomas 23

Phillips,Bernard T. 31;Lucinda 29;Sally 31

Pinn,Mary 31

Pinckard,Edward 50,61;James 12; Jedithen 11;Nancy H. *40;Thomas 15,40

Pitman,Catharine 30;Cyrus 50,53, 60,62,63,64;Edward C. *35,58; George,Jr. 22,*24,25,34,*35; Isaac *30,48,53;Leroy M. 27; Nancy 30;Robert 64;Thomas 14,30; William 19,35,45,48,50,59,64;

Plunket,James 53

Pointer,Henry 11

Pollard,Betsy 37;Catharine 40; Catharine P. 40;Clarissa 37; James 2,3,14,40;Nancy H. 40; Sally 37,38;Sarah Ann 40;Thomas 4,20,*21,37;Capt.Thomas *27,31, *32;William *40,44

Porter,Elizabeth 41,43;William 41, 43

Potts,Francis 63,64

Pullen(Pullin)George 45,52,60; Henry 29,48;James 16;Jonathan 10;William 48,54,60

Rains(Raines)Alfrod J. 28,50; Albert J. 61;Eliza 28;Raleigh 48;Richard 28;Robert L.28; Susan 28;Thomas S. 28;Warner J. 28;William C. 28

Rant(Rout?)Richard 48

Reaves,Elizabeth 29;James 29; Lucinda 29

Rew,Daniel 49

Rice,John 48,49

Richard,Edward 48

Richardson,John 48,50,51,53

Richinson,John 55

Richson,John 49

Riveer(Rivier-Riviere),Bushrod 14;Cyrus 64;James 14,64;Joel 64;John 14;Johnson 16;Peter 16;William 14,63,*64

Robb,Thomas 11,12

Robbins,Mary E. 42;William 42

Robinson(Robertson)Andrew 48, 63;Catharine 39;Cyrus 26; Eleazer 15;Elijah 16;James 48,61;Jesse *14;Lemuel 48

Robertson(Robinson)Andrew 13; Dr. Andrew 16;Cyrus 59,60; Robert M. 58;Thomas G.63;

Roberts,Capt.Cyrus L.30;George 48;John 12,53,57;Lorenzo 30;

Rogers(Rodgers)Charles 12; Hannah 29;John *25,*29,44,58

Nancy 29;Nathaniel C. 29;Richard 25;William H. 44,62

Rock,William 31

Ruse,Daniel 48

Routt(Rant),Richard 64;Willoughby 16

Samuel,Michael 50

Sampson,John 48,62

Saunders,Betty 14;Elizabeth 9; Presly 4

Schofield(Scofield)Henry 48,53,57; John 54,57;Thos: 48,49,51,55; William 11,15

Sebrie(Sebre),John 16;Nicholas 50

Sebria,Cordelia 29;Travis 29

Selden,Capt. 4;James *1;John 4,16, 18;Mary 16;Richard *2,3,16,19

Shelton,Daniel 48,51,53,62

Shanglan(Straughan)Elizabeth T. 27

Shearman,Ann 10;Capt. *62;Hannah M. *28;Joseph 1,9,17,44,57,58; Rawleigh 18;Samuel M. 28,44,53,55, 56;Thomas 62;Thomas W.M. 28

Short,Moses 53,57,62,64

Sims,William 63,64

Simmons(Simmonds)Charles 50,53,57,62; James 12,15;John 48;William 48,61

Smith,Alice 11,15,20;George 48,50,60; John M. 50;John N. 60;Spencer 64; Spencer C. 53,57;William 3

Spermane,George 48

Spilman,George 53,62;William 48,54

Spriggs,Betsey W. 28,40;Nathan *28,*40;Polly 28,40

Stamper,Leonard 45

Stanham,Samuel 48,62

Stephens,Ann 10;Joseph 16; William 14

Steinway,Hugh 34;Sarah Ann 34

Stoneham,Samuel 50

Stott,Archibald *40;Eppa 19; John 45;Sarah Ann 40;Thomas 8;William 11,14,61

Straughan(Shanglan)Alice 38; Elizabeth 38;Jane 38;Mary 38; Martha W. *38;Samuel L. *38

Sullivant(Sullivan)Ahimes 64; Cornelius 58;John 4

Summers,Hugh 42;Sarah Ann 42

Sutton,James 45;William 48,50

Sydnor,Fortunatus 9,15;William 11,16;William B. 48,59

Taff,John 45,63

Talley,Champn: 50;George 48,62; James 61;John 62;Thomas I(J?) 48,62

Talman(Toleman-Toalman)John 48, 53,64;Joseph 51,55

Tankersley,James 48;James R.51; Thornley 48,49;Thornley B. 55; Thomly B. 50;Thornton B. 51

Tapscott,Edney 10,16;Ellis L.B. 51,56;David H. 59;Henry 1,14, 48,62;James 9,17,18,20;James W. 50;John M.S. 53;Mary 10; Rawleigh 2,*5,*6,*7,*8,*9,*10, *11,*12,*13,16,17,*21;Warner L.

59,62

Tapore, Betsy 30; John *30

Tarpley, John 13

Taylor, Col. 8; Col. John 6,7,10, 11,*13,15,17; Maj. John *1,*2, 4,*14,*16; Rich^d 13;

Thatcher, Hannah 3,23,24,*25,26; William 4,23,24,*25,26

Thomas, Amos 22; George 48,50,63,64; John 59,60; Tarpley 22; Thomsey R. 29; V. *63; Vinvent 64

Thornton, Col. Peter P. 9

Thrall, Ann 33; James 52,56; John *33,45,51,56; Judith 33; Thomas 48,50; William 48,53,57

Towell(Towill), Richard 48,51,56; Thomas 53,54

Towles, H. 13; Henry 1,*4,*6,13, 18,21; Lt. Henry 25; Paktues 48,54,58,60

Tilman(Tillman), Isaac 53; P. 10

Treacle(Treackle-Treackly-Treckley), Dempsey 48,53,57; John *42; Juliet Ann *42; Rich'd. 57 Samuel 57

Wall(Wale), George 58; Samuel 64

Wale(Wall), George 51,55

Wallace, James 9,15

Walker, Benjamin 62; John 48,64; Thos 9

Warren, William 11,16

Warwick, James 48,60; Thomas L. 48; Thomas S. 59

Watts, Spencer 64; William 50;

William L. 58

Weaver, Betty 30; Betsey 31; Elijah *31; John 30

Weadon, Gen. 7

Webb, George 50,58; Griffin 60; John 17

Welsh, George 48; Griffin 48

Wessels, Custis 38,41; Nancy 38,41

West, Joseph 50,59

Wheeler, Maurice 14

Wiblin(Weblin)Esther 22; William 11,22; Williamson 59,60

Wilson, Cyrus 29,33,59,60; Cyrus L. 30; Elizabeth 33; John *29, *30,*33; Joseph 31; Judith 39; Martin 39; Samuel 33; William *30

Wilder, John 48,53,57; Jonathan 11; Michael 1

Wilkins, James W. 31; Polly H. 31

Wilkerson, Joseph 14

Williams, Charles 15; Elizabeth 29

Wirt, Joseph 45

Wood, James 25; Mary 31; Thomas 16

Wormeley 7

Yerby, Charles 54,58; Charles J. 61,62; Elizabeth 29; Elizabeth 33; George 19; John 48,51,52,53; Judith 11,15; Thomas 44,53,56; Capt. Thomas 57,*61,*62; William 2,4,18; William T. 44; Capt. Wm. T. *61,*62

Yopp, Samuel 13; William 10
Young, Rich^d 17

www.ingramcontent.com/pod-product-compliance
Lightning Source LLC
Chambersburg PA
CBHW051703090426
42736CB00013B/2519